CREATIVE
INDUSTRIES

Practical guides for practical people. In this increasingly sophisticated world the need for manually skilled people to build our homes, cut our hair, fix our boilers, and make our cars go is greater than ever. As things progress, so the level of training and competence required of our skilled manual workers increases.

In this new series of career guides from Trotman, we look in detail at what it takes to train for, get into, and be successful at a wide spectrum of practical careers. *Real Life Guides* aim to inform and inspire young people and adults alike by providing comprehensive yet hard-hitting and often blunt information about what it takes to succeed in these careers.

Other titles in the series are:
THE ARMED FORCES
THE BEAUTY INDUSTRY
BUSINESS, ADMINISTRATION & FINANCE
CARE
CARPENTRY & CABINET-MAKING
CATERING
CHILDCARE
CONSTRUCTION
DISTRIBUTION & LOGISTICS
ELECTRICIAN
ENGINEERING TECHNICIAN
THE FIRE SERVICE
HAIRDRESSING
HOSPITALITY & EVENTS MANAGEMENT
INFORMATION & COMMUNICATIONS TECHNOLOGY
THE MOTOR INDUSTRY
PLUMBING
THE POLICE SERVICE
RETAILING
REAL SPORT & ACTIVE LEISURE
TRANSPORT
TRAVEL & TOURISM
WORKING OUTDOORS
WORKING WITH ANIMALS & WILDLIFE
WORKING WITH YOUNG PEOPLE

trotman

REAL life
GUIDES

CREATIVE INDUSTRIES

KAREN HOLMES

Real Life Guide to Creative Industries

This first edition is published in 2009 by Trotman, an imprint of Crimson Publishing, Westminster House, Kew Road, Richmond, Surrey TW9 2ND.

© Trotman Publishing 2009

Author: Karen Holmes

British Library Cataloguing in Publication Data
A catalogue record for this book is available from the British Library

ISBN: 978-1-84455-223-8

Typeset by RefineCatch Limited, Bungay, Suffolk

Printed and bound in Italy by LEGO SpA Ltd

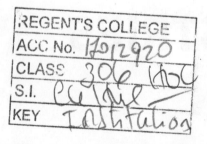

CONTENTS

FOREWORD

This *Real Life Guide to Creative Industries* offers practical information on every aspect of training for and finding a job in the field. Whether you are just starting out or looking for your next career move this book shows the different entry routes into the industry, gives you an outline of the jobs available, and explains the skills and attributes you need to be successful.

City & Guilds vocational qualifications support learners from pre-entry to professional level and we award over a million certificates every year. Our qualifications meet the latest industry requirements and are recognised by employers worldwide as proof that candidates have the knowledge and skills to get the job done.

We are delighted to be a part of the Trotman *Real Life Guides* series to help raise your awareness of these vocational qualifications – we are confident that they can help you to achieve excellence and quality in whichever field you choose. For more information about the courses City & Guilds offer check out www.cityandguilds.com – get yourself qualified and see what you could do.

City & Guilds

ABOUT THE AUTHOR

Karen Holmes is a freelance writer specialising in education, management and training. She has written a number of careers books, as well as articles for magazines and journals on career development. She has also prepared a range of resources designed to support the 14–19 Diploma in Creative and Media, and is the author of *Design Uncovered*, a careers title published by Trotman.

ACKNOWLEDGEMENTS

Many thanks to all the people who contributed to this book by describing their work and experiences, particularly DJ Z, Ellie Poole and Neela Patel. Also, thanks to Elizabeth Rafii-Tabar at Trotman for her careful editing and useful suggestions, all of which were much appreciated.

INTRODUCTION

Unless you're very wealthy – or have already decided to drop out of the material world – at some point soon you're going to start thinking about your future career. The choices you make, particularly when you're starting out in the world of work, are very important and can influence the rest of your life. So you need to consider your options carefully and start doing some research.

Some people's career choices are driven by a desire for wealth or financial security, some want recognition, some want to help others. Then there are the people (and you are probably one of them if you've picked up this book) who know that they'll only really be happy if they have a job that relates to their creative talents and interests. These people (you?) don't necessarily want to star in a blockbuster movie or win the *X Factor*. They just know that they want to contribute to the making of something – whether that's a sculpture, a computer game, a wrought iron gate or a piece of clothing.

The government estimated that in 2007 there were nearly two million people involved in creative employment. Some of these

---

JARGON BUSTER

Create (*verb*): to cause to come into existence.
Creative (*adjective*): having the ability to create; characterised by originality of thought; having or showing imagination.

---

people are performers and artisans – but many more work 'behind the scenes'. These individuals have found practical ways to combine their skills and creative talents in a competitive employment arena.

WHAT ARE THE 'CREATIVE INDUSTRIES'?

This term applies to work that is based on individual creativity, skill and talent. It's an important area of employment not only because it gives people a chance to use their abilities and find fulfilling careers, but also because it generates a lot of money for the country's economy. Here in the UK we like our creative pursuits; thousands of us visit theatres, cinemas and live music festivals, we love craft and antique fairs, we have a reputation as one of the great fashion and music centres in the world.

DID YOU KNOW?

UK households spend an average of £59 each week on recreation and culture – more than on any other commodities and services except transport!

Our creative industries are also respected overseas. We export our music, fashion, artwork, crafts, computer games and films worldwide and this again generates money: in 2004, our creative industries exports totalled £13 billion – 4.3% of all goods and services exported from the UK.

The Department of Culture, Media and Sports identifies a number of sectors as 'creative industries'. We can't cover all of them in detail in this book, so we're focusing on these seven:

1. arts and antiques
2. crafts
3. designer fashion

4. film, video and photography
5. software, computer games and electronic publishing
6. music and the visual and performing arts
7. television and radio.

Because the term 'creative industries' covers a wide spectrum of career opportunities it's hard to make generalisations. Yes, some sectors like the performing arts, music and designer fashion are notoriously hard to get started in. For every Daniel Radcliffe, Lady Gaga and Alexander McQueen, there are a hundred thousand 'wannabes'. But other creative industry sectors, such as software, computer games, TV and radio have expanded rapidly during the last ten years and now offer many opportunities for talented, dedicated individuals at all levels. To put it simply, you may not get a chance to play the part of Doctor Who, but you could find a rewarding and satisfying career as part of its production team!

DID YOU KNOW?

In 2008, government research identified 157,400 businesses in the creative industries.

WHAT'S IN THIS BOOK FOR ME?

Getting a job that uses our creative talents is a dream that many of us have and few of us achieve. Nevertheless, if you have talent, skill and are willing to work hard, there are career opportunities out there. This book will help you to access some of them.

We look at a number of different career opportunities in the creative industries, discuss what the work involves and what skills and competences, education and training you'll need to access these. Our focus is on jobs that are available to non-graduates, so you'll find it particularly useful if you're considering starting your working life when you leave school or college.

DID YOU KNOW?

Creative industries have existed for thousands of years because people have always wanted to express their feelings by creating things. The Egyptians were making musical instruments (harps) in 3000BC – and that's just one example of their many skilled craft industries. Some experts believe that the first painted or engraved signs were made 40,000 years ago, thus signalling the beginning of the art 'industry'!

In Chapter 2 we examine the current state of the creative sectors and look at the number of people who work in different parts of the industry. It's always been difficult to get a break in the performing arts, TV, fashion, etc. Is it getting harder, or are creative people finding that there is a still a demand for their talents?

In Chapter 3, 'What Are the Jobs?', we introduce you to a selection of roles in the creative industries. Obviously we can't cover everything, but all the jobs that we've profiled offer ways into different sectors if you are starting your career straight after leaving school or college.

Chapter 5 considers the skills and attributes you need to succeed in the jobs that we've selected. The information in this section will be useful even if you're not sure which career path you want to follow because it outlines the personal, technical and business skills that are useful within a particular industry sector.

In Chapter 6 we answer some of the most frequently asked questions about working in the creative industries, and Chapter 8 gives information about relevant training and qualifications.

Chapter 9, 'The Last Word', summarises some of things you've discovered about careers in the creative industries and asks you to complete a brief self-assessment quiz to find out if this is the right career path for you.

In Chapters 1, 4 and 7 we've included a success story and case studies about individuals who are working in their chosen fields. These give a real flavour of what the different jobs involve – and hopefully will encourage you to explore creative career opportunities yourself.

CHAPTER 1
SUCCESS STORY

DJ Z

Music producer

We've included a number of case studies in this book to introduce you to individuals who've established successful careers in different sectors of the creative industries.

This success story explores the career of DJ Z (pronounced *dee-jay-ʒee*). Z is a 25-year-old music producer and DJ, based in London. He has recently started his own recording label so that he can develop new talent.

'From my early teens I was passionate about music and started developing my DJ-ing skills and producing demo CDs that I sent to both large recording companies and small independent labels. I never got any feedback, but at least I got into the habit of sending them off – you have to be persistent in this business.

'I liked school but I wasn't very academic and I knew early on that I didn't want to go to university. I was lucky that my mum and dad were happy to support me as long as I was doing *something*. I did seven GCSEs, including Music, IT and Design and Technology. Then I went to the local further education college and did a one-year course in music technology. Even though I already knew a lot of the technical stuff, it helped to focus me and I learned to use my skills for a real purpose rather than just messing around. I had a part-time job, too – working as a cleaner in a nightclub. Don't laugh! The work might not have been very exciting – and sometimes it was pretty revolting – but I made my first contacts there. The resident DJ helped me a lot and persuaded the manager to let me have a couple of trials.

'I got my first club residency when I was 17; it was one night a week in another local place but it really helped develop my skills and I learned to read an audience and know what they wanted. I got together with a techie friend who built me a website and we got into MySpace and YouTube very early on so I could showcase my work.

'About a year later, one of the labels followed up on a demo I'd sent to them and that was the break I needed. Soon after that I had an agent, a recording contract and was playing in venues all over the country. A couple of years later, I decided I wanted to start my own label so that I could hothouse new acts that I liked.

'I rent studio space when I'm recording and work with engineers and sound technicians that I know and trust – that makes a big difference. I've made a lot of music industry connections so I'm finding the promotion side easier – I can get a foot in the door when I want people to listen to a new act.

'I'm doing something that I love but it's also hard work and you've got to be prepared for that. I think a lot of people are more in love with the idea of celebrity than the graft that's involved in being a good musician. On a typical day, I deal with admin and any queries or feedback on my website in the morning, and talk to people like my agent and accountant. There's always a lot of checking to do before a tour to make sure that everything is in place – and I'm still at the stage where I do a lot of it myself. Maybe when I'm really successful I can employ some assistants to do the legwork!

'I try to spend most afternoons when I'm in the studio either on my own stuff or with acts that I'm interested in. Evenings I'm usually working, and if there's any spare time I try to study. I'm doing a book-keeping and accounting course. I know that doesn't sound very rock and roll but it's easy to get ripped off if you don't understand the basics and keep a close eye on your money. There's a lot of technology involved in my work so I have to keep abreast of that – although I'm not studying a formal music technology course at the moment, I spend a few hours a week with a friend who keeps me up to speed.

'This is a great business to be in, but I'd be lying if I said it was easy to break into. You need to be passionate about your music so that you can put up with the knock backs and you have to be really persistent – I sent off dozens of demos before I got so much as a whisper of interest. I think you need a head for business as well. People get the idea that the music industry is all about glamour and creativity but the bottom line is money – it's there to make a profit. The more you understand about contracts, publishing, copyright and finance, the easier it will be for you to survive.

'Careers in the creative industries – particularly if you want to perform in some way – are tricky. But those of us who succeed are really driven and we know that we couldn't do anything else. That says it all, really.'

CHAPTER 2
WHAT ARE THE CREATIVE INDUSTRIES?

In this chapter we give an overview of the creative industries and look in more detail at the sectors that feature in this book. How many people are employed in these sectors? Are the different sectors expanding or contracting – and how will this affect the job market? Read on and find out.

DREAMS AND REALITY

Most of us have a creative talent of some kind. We might be good at singing, dancing or acting. We may be talented artists, sculptors or woodcarvers. Some of us know that we could design better products like computer games, clothes and television programmes than the ones that we see around us. But only a very few of us will be able to turn our creative talent into a career. And even fewer of us will make that career a financial success.

It's only fair in a book like this that we tell you the facts: the creative industries are the hardest to get into and the ones that most people are forced to leave after a short time because they can't earn enough money to survive. We might dream about winning *Britain's Got Talent* or the Turner Prize, but the chances of doing so are one in a million. There are simply too many people in the creative industries chasing too few opportunities.

That's the bad news. The good news is that if you have a creative talent and enough determination, you *will* succeed. People who make a successful career in the creative industries are driven by the knowledge that they really don't want to do anything else, so they're willing to work hard and put up with the setbacks to achieve their goal.

They're also willing to rethink their definition of 'a successful career'. Success isn't always about making a lot of money or being famous – it's about doing something that you love, that makes you want to get up in the morning and hurry into work. Many people who work in the antiques trade, TV and film industries, performing arts and the other creative industries live on a shoestring but they have immense job satisfaction. They may have low-profile jobs, but they consider themselves to be successful because they are happy with their careers.

If you're reading this book because you really want to use your talent as the basis of your career, then you'll be prepared for a lot of hard work, low pay and masses of competition. None of which will put you off, because you know that you won't be truly happy working in any other field.

EMPLOYMENT PROSPECTS

In this book, we're focusing on seven sectors of the creative industries. Before we start looking at different types of jobs, it's worth examining the current state of play in these sectors.

According to government statistics, there were nearly two million people involved in creative employment in 2007. More than 1,147,000 were working in the creative industries, and the remaining 830,000 were in creative occupations outside the creative industries (for example, creatives employed by large corporations such as banks to carry out particular types of work).

In this chapter, we'll give you a whistle-stop tour of seven sectors in the creative industries that you may be interested in. All of them offer career opportunities at different levels, from school-leaver to graduate entry.

Arts and antiques

The UK has a long tradition of producing high quality art and fine goods. Artists such as Gainsborough and Reynolds were major influences on portrait painting in the eighteenth century; Constable and Turner are two of the most famous landscape artists in the world, and artists like David Hockney, Damien Hurst and Antony Gormley are now leading figures in contemporary art.

Many British artists have also been leaders in international art and craft movements. Among them are pottery designer Clarice Cliff, famous as an exponent of Art Deco, and Charles Rennie Mackintosh, renowned for his Art Nouveau designs for both the exterior and interior of buildings.

Furniture designers such as Thomas Chippendale and George Hepplewhite, who both worked in the eighteenth century, helped to establish a thriving industry in fine furniture manufacture. Part of their legacy – and that of other artists and craftspeople – has been to establish the UK as a major centre for the arts and antiques trade. Collectors come here from all over the world to find the treasures that they seek.

Of all the creative industries that we're exploring in this book, arts and antiques employ the least number of people: 21,800 in 2007. Generally, this is a sector that is dominated by small businesses – many art galleries and antique outlets will only employ two or three people.

The number of businesses (1,600) in this sector remained pretty static over a 10-year period up to 2008. At the moment, business is not brilliant – arts and antiques are primarily businesses that sell luxury items, and people have less money to spend on non-essentials in times of economic downturn. However, and it's an important point to remember if you're thinking about a career in this sector, art and antiques can be useful investments. When bank interest rates are low, some wealthy people will put their money into valuable goods such as paintings, silver, furniture, etc. and wait for their value to increase. So although the sector may be experiencing some difficulties, there will always be a market for high-quality items – and reputable antique and art dealers will stay in business.

Q DID YOU KNOW?

The fine-art saleroom Christie's is the oldest in the world. It was founded in London in 1766 by an Australian-born auctioneer, James Christie.

The sector has also been transformed in recent years by the internet. Big auction houses such as Sotheby's and Christie's allow customers to view and take part in live auctions by streaming them online. You could be at home in London taking part in an auction in New York! Customers can also browse upcoming items for future auctions and create a personal account online of all the auctions selling items of particular interest.

Crafts

There's an old saying that Britain is a nation of shopkeepers; we could equally be described as a nation of craftspeople. From seventeenth-century printmaker and engraver William Hogarth to pottery manufacturer Josiah Wedgwood, we've produced generations of talented individuals who make truly original and desirable objects.

In 2007, there were 109,700 people working in the craft sector, earning a living by using different materials and skills to produce objects. Here are just some of the types of craft that people are involved in: bookbinding, candlemaking, ceramics, furniture making, glass production, jewellery making, metal working, musical instrument making, stone carving, wood turning and sculpture. Craftspeople also make new clothes using recycled textiles, make toys, practise lettering and calligraphy, produce decorative mirrors – the list of different types of craft that people have developed into careers is very, very long!

Some craftspeople work alone in a studio in their home; others are members of craft co-operatives who have joined together to hire premises and sell their products collectively. The markets they sell to also vary enormously; obviously many are sold through craft shops and small retail outlets, but large department stores will also commission individual or limited edition pieces if they think they will appeal to customers.

The internet has revolutionised marketing in the craft sector. There are now well-established websites such as Etsy and Folksy that offer craftspeople a shop window for their goods. These offer newcomers a great chance to test the popularity of their goods in the open market before they commit themselves to a career choice. So, if you have a real talent for making craft items, these are sites where you can find out if anyone wants to buy them. Keep up to date on the internet because new marketplace sites are opening all the time – but check the small print carefully before you offer your products for sale to confirm commission charges and to make sure that the site is legitimate!

In the same way that there will be a market for antiques and collectables, there will also be one for craft items because almost everyone likes beautiful or unusual objects.

Designer fashion

The UK has been a major influence on the fashion world since the eighteenth century, partly because of the Industrial Revolution when new machinery was introduced to process wool and cotton. With mass production of cheap fabrics came new designs for clothes – many of which originated in this country. We have a reputation for producing innovative designers, from

DID YOU KNOW?

The first dressmaker to open a fashion house in the rue de la Paix in Paris was Charles Worth – an Englishman – in 1858.

Mary Quant in the 1960s to Vivienne Westwood and Alexander McQueen today.

If you looked at the increase in the number of designer fashion businesses between 2007 and 2008 (up from 1,700 to 2,800) you could be forgiven for thinking that this sector is booming. Read the small print, however, and you'll see that the massive increase is because of a change in the way that the statistics are calculated rather than a sudden massive demand for high fashion!

Designer fashion is not just about clothes – there is a huge market for accessories, shoes and textiles. Not all would-be fashion designers will become as famous as Stella McCartney – but this sector employs a lot of people in support roles, from machinists who make up clothes to stylists who help present them for catwalk shows and photo shoots.

Approximately 90,000 people are employed in the UK in the manufacture of clothing and other textile-related goods. Although the manufacture of clothes, shoes and textiles is increasingly done overseas where labour is cheaper, the UK still has a significant clothing and textile industry producing 'high-end' goods.

Film, video and photography

The film production industry didn't really develop in this country until the 1930s – by which time Hollywood was already established as the home of the movies. By 1927, such a low percentage of films shown in cinemas were British that the government passed the Cinematograph Films Act. This forced the cinemas to show more locally made films and helped to establish some of the great British production studios such as Pinewood, Elstree and Shepperton. The 1940s was the golden age of British cinema but

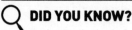

DID YOU KNOW?

One location that has become a centre for film making in recent years is the Isle of Man.

after that the industry declined until the early 1980s, when *Chariots of Fire* (1981) started a revival, particularly of historical and 'period' films.

DID YOU KNOW?

In 2006, the UK film industry contributed £4.3 billion to the UK economy.

Today the British film industry is well regarded across the world. In recent years, with massively successful productions such as *Slumdog Millionaire* and the recent James Bond and Harry Potter movies, it's been dominating the headlines once again. We're currently responsible for about 20% of all new film releases.

It's difficult to get reliable facts and figures for this sector because many production companies have a short lifespan; they are set up while a film is made and then closed down. There are approximately 400 registered (i.e. permanent) companies in the film industry. Approximately 43% of these are involved in development, production and providing facilities, 13% in distribution and the remaining 44% in exhibiting and exporting films.

Software, computer games and electronic publishing

Of all the sectors in the creative industries, this is the one that is currently experiencing the most growth – and will probably go on doing so. Consequently, it offers some of the best job opportunities. More than 640,000 people currently work in this field; it is by far the biggest employer of all the creative industries that we're looking at in this book.

DID YOU KNOW?

The UK computer games market is the third largest in the world after those in the US and Japan and has the highest number of games development companies and publishers in Europe. There are approximately 150 development studios operating in the UK, employing 6,000 people, and in 2006 the UK computer games industry recorded sales of £1.6 billion.

The popularity of home computing exploded in the 1980s, bringing a huge demand for both business and entertainment software. Sales of entertainment software now outstrip both the DVD rental market and cinema box office spending. One of the reasons for this is that the sector is constantly changing. It attracts innovators who continually want to push technical boundaries – so almost every month there's a new product on the market. Many of these, such as the Wii and interactive mobile phones, rapidly become 'must haves'.

Many people see electronic publishing as a major new growth area. Hand-held monitors on which you can read a book may not replace the printed word for everyone, but they are gaining a foothold in the market. There's also an increasing demand for hardware and software that allow people to produce their own books or have books printed on demand.

If you're interested in technology and have the necessary skills and aptitudes for working in this sector, the prospects for the future are good. Even in an economic downturn, the buying public is unlikely to lose its thirst for technology.

Music and the visual and performing arts

The UK is home to some of the greatest classical musicians and orchestras in the world, and thousands of people attend concerts and events such as the Proms and Glyndebourne. We're also recognised as a country where new, contemporary talent is encouraged. Punk, Prog-rock, Glam Rock, Two Tone, New

Romanticism and Britpop are all movements that have thrived over the last few decades.

It may be more than 40 years since The Beatles started a worldwide passion for British contemporary music, but we're still at the cutting edge of music production. Our artists, composers, producers, managers, music publishers, concert promoters and agents, record companies, and online music entrepreneurs are respected worldwide.

As a nation, we love to buy and download music – we're the third largest market in the world for sales of music. That helps to make the music industry one of the UK's biggest players in the national economy, contributing nearly £5 billion annually and employing more than 262,000 people. This sector is still remarkably healthy; it may not be easy to break into but once you've made your mark, the employment opportunities are many and varied.

The UK music industry is determined to stay at the cutting edge. It invests proportionately more in research and development than the aerospace, defence, car and computer industries!

The performing arts offer more than the chance to shine on stage as an actor, musician or dancer. For every performer working in this sector, there are a dozen people working backstage – directors, choreographers, musical arrangers, costume and make-up artists, stage hands, lighting and sound technicians, promoters, theatre and venue managers… Some are employed by large organisations such as repertory companies or performance venues like O2, but many others work for small companies.

DID YOU KNOW?

There are 5,350 businesses in the performing arts sector. 88% of them employ fewer than five people. In total 84,470 people are employed in the sector.

This will always be a competitive sector to get into and one that is rife with job insecurity. However, that doesn't put off the thousands of new entrants every year. If you have sufficient talent to work 'front of stage' or the enthusiasm and skills to contribute backstage, you'll find an opening somewhere – just be prepared to work hard to find it.

Television and radio

The world's first public television service started from the BBC station at Alexandra Palace in North London in November 1936. It had a huge impact on the country; in the early days when few people had TV sets, many families would cram into a house to watch major televised events such as the Queen's coronation in 1953 and the funeral of Winston Churchill in 1965.

Today many households have more than one TV and very few of us don't spend at least some part of our day in front of 'the box'. To satisfy demand there are now dozens of television and radio companies. As well as the terrestrial broadcasters such as the BBC, ITV, Channel 4 and Channel Five, there are also hundreds of cable and satellite broadcasters like BSkyB, Virgin Media and Disney.

Q DID YOU KNOW?

The UK radio industry has been growing in recent years and now employs more than 22,000 people in a wide range of occupations.

Recently, there has been a notable growth in the number of community and special interest TV companies that broadcast programmes to minority groups, ranging from ethnic minorities to professionals such as teachers. Supplying the various television and radio companies with programmes are around 1,500 independent production companies, varying in size from the big names like Tiger Aspect to small indies (independent film companies).

Job prospects in this sector are being affected by major changes in public attitudes to home entertainment. Most TV and radio companies are funded by money that advertisers pay in order to air their ads. As more and more of us access programmes via the internet, advertising income for the terrestrial and digital broadcasters is falling and this is affecting the number of programmes that can be made. However, as the big broadcasting and production companies face cuts this may open up new opportunities for smaller, independent production companies. Employees may have to rethink the way that they work, however, and be prepared for greater flexibility as they move from one short contract to another.

DID YOU KNOW?

In 2004/5 there were 180,000 courses in creative and cultural-related fields and more than half a million further and higher education students – but there were only 6,000 new vacancies advertised in the creative and cultural industries. Do the maths!

WHAT'S THE PROBLEM?

The biggest problem facing someone like you, who wants a career in the creative industries, is knowing where to begin. Unlike professions such as teaching, the law or engineering, there is no formal education and training structure for getting into this field. You're as likely to get a job because of *who* you know (i.e. your contacts and network of friends and colleagues) as *what* you know (i.e. your educational background).

WHAT'S THE SOLUTION?

There are no easy answers, but reading this book is a good start to finding a way into the creative industries. It will help to:

▶ prepare you for the (sometimes difficult) path you've chosen
▶ select appropriate training and educational opportunities
▶ recognise the skills you need, as well as your creative talent, to build a successful career.

Before you move on, try the following short quiz to find out how much you know about the creative industries.

QUIZ

Are you well-informed about the creative industries – or do you need to broaden your knowledge? Try our quiz to find out.

1 **If you got a job as a 'runner' you'd expect to work:**
   A. As a driver in the antiques trade?
   B. As a junior employee on a film or TV production?
   C. As a seamstress making clothes?
   D. In electronic publishing?

2 **The National Trust is a:**
   A. Bank?
   B. Museum?
   C. Heritage organisation?
   D. School for antique restorers?

3 **In your job, you often use prosthetics. You are a:**
   A. Computer games programmer?
   B. Fashion designer?
   C. TV camera operator?
   D. Make-up artist?

4 **The Turner Prize is awarded for:**
   A. Visual arts?
   B. Literature?
   C. Music?
   D. Performing arts?

5 **Dreamweaver is:**
   A. A type of computer software?
   B. A weaving frame for fabrics?
   C. An electronic keyboard for making music?
   D. A computer game?

6 Calligraphy is a craft based on:
A. Woodcarving?
B. Weaving?
C. Lettering?
D. Paper folding?

7 A plugger:
A. Makes wigs and hair pieces?
B. Promotes new records and bands?
C. Renovates and restores old kitchen equipment?
D. Acts as a prompter for stage productions?

8 RADA is:
A. A leading drama school?
B. A government communications agency?
C. A band?
D. A process for editing video?

9 Alexander McQueen is a famous:
A. TV producer?
B. Sculptor?
C. Musician?
D. Fashion designer?

10 An Assembler is:
A. A computer game?
B. A computer programming language?
C. A type of personal computer?
D. A computer operating system?

ANSWERS

1. B. A runner does basic tasks like fetching and carrying, making the tea and delivering scripts on TV and film productions. Many people who go on to become successful producers and directors get their first job as a runner. You'll find out more about this work in Chapter 3, 'What Are the Jobs?'.
2. C. The National Trust is a heritage organisation. Founded in 1895 to preserve land and buildings of historic interest, it owns and cares for many famous stately homes, houses, gardens, open land and coastline across the UK.
3. D. You are a make-up artist. Prosthetics are items such as false noses and scars, wigs and hair decorations that are used to change a person's appearance.
4. A. The Turner Prize is awarded for visual arts. It is awarded every year to a British artist under the age of 50 whose work is considered to be outstanding.
5. A. Dreamweaver is a type of computer software.
6. C. Calligraphy is the art of handwriting. Despite the development of computer software that can produce decorative print, calligraphers are still used to produce decorative handwriting for certificates, letters, invitations, etc.
7. B. A plugger promotes music. The work involves taking records to radio producers and DJs and persuading them to play them on air, and contacting other forms of media to ask for reviews and mentions.
8. A. RADA is the Royal Academy of Dramatic Arts. Founded in 1904 to train young actors, it is now considered to be one of the world's leading drama schools.
9. D. Alexander McQueen is a famous fashion designer.
10. B. Assembler is a computer programming language.

CHAPTER 3
WHAT ARE THE JOBS?

There are hundreds of different jobs in the creative industries and there's no way that we can cover them all in a book of this length. In this chapter we examine a few specific roles in each sector to give you a flavour of the types of work available. We've focused primarily on non-graduate jobs where you may need some practical training before you start, but your career isn't dependent on a specific academic qualification.

You will notice that some sections in this chapter cover a broader range of jobs than others. This is because the industries covered in this book vary enormously in size. The art and antiques sector in particular is very small. Each section will show you a range of jobs for each sector but some will have more than others.

ARTS AND ANTIQUES

There is a wide range of jobs associated with arts and antiques, even though the number of people employed in this sector is quite small. Here are a few examples.

Saleroom porter

Saleroom porters work in auction houses. Their work involves moving around goods that have been put in for sale, arranging them for display and showing them to the bidders during the auction. If you've watched TV programmes like *Cash in the Attic* or *Flog It!*, you'll have seen them in action. Many porters get a chance to move up in the business, learning how to compile inventories of stock and catalogues, research items, give valuations and work with customers.

Antiques dealer

Dealers buy and sell goods that other people will collect. Although to be officially classified as an antique, an item has to be over 100 years old, some dealers specialise in more recent 'collectables' such as furniture and jewellery from the 1920s and 1930s. They may sell their goods in shops, galleries, fairs, auction houses, on the internet and even at car boot sales. Dealers need to be knowledgeable about the goods that they specialise in so that they can recognise them, vouch for their authenticity and – most importantly – put a realistic value on them. Another important part of their work is giving valuations so that owners can insure their property.

Museum/art gallery attendant

This is a great career for friendly, outgoing people who like working with the public and have a passion for history and/or art. Attendants answer queries and provide information, and in some places provide guided tours where they tell visitors about what is on display. They are also responsible for safety and security. At a higher level, some people who want to work in this field become curators who manage and maintain collections of art or historical objects. This job usually demands specialist knowledge and relevant qualifications, such as a degree in History or Fine Art.

Other jobs in arts and antiques include:

- ▶ restoring antiques and paintings so that any faults or defects are repaired
- ▶ making reproduction antiques and copying artworks (note that this is legal as long as you don't try to pass off reproductions as the real thing!)
- ▶ finding specific items for collectors
- ▶ working in museums and stately homes, helping to conserve items so that they remain in good condition.

There are two basic criteria for building a career in arts and antiques.

▶ A passion for beautiful things; if you're going to convince potential customers to buy something that you are selling or restoring, you have to genuinely care about it

▶ Knowledge about your chosen field. There are so many different types of artwork and antiques that you will need to specialise in a particular area and learn everything you can about it. So, for example, you may work primarily with antique silver, modern paintings, eighteenth-century furniture, Turkish rugs, etc. Antiques and art dealers rely on their expertise in spotting quality items that they can sell for a profit – and you will only build up this expertise if you focus your attention on a specific area.

PROFILE

Sarah is a self-employed antique dealer. Here she describes how her career developed.

'I started buying and selling antiques by accident when I was still at sixth-form college – my family was having a clear out and I took it to a car-boot sale. That gave me the bug so I started looking for small items to buy, then sold them on at flea markets. I was still selling a wide range of low-value goods but I'd started collecting silver sugar tongs because I liked them. Over a period of a couple of years, what started as a hobby became a full-time job. I studied silver, learned about hallmarks and how to value pieces, partly through books and also by working unpaid for a local antique dealer one day a week. He taught me a lot. At the same time I was picking up essential business skills like how to keep the books and market my stock. I was still trading at fairs and also started selling pieces on the internet, and did quite well. Last year, I rented a stand in an antique emporium so I now have a permanent base where customers can find me – even though a lot of my business is still done online. I have a number of regular customers who come to me when they want something special.'

Getting a first job can be difficult because vacancies are rarely advertised. You need to keep your eyes and ears open and make as many contacts as you can by attending sales and fairs. This is one business where it is acceptable simply to 'knock on doors'; try approaching antique shops and asking if they have any work available. Be prepared for very low salaries or only to earn commission on things that you sell.

Once you've started work in the sector, however, increasing your experience gets much easier. Arts and antiques are fields where everyone seems to know everyone else and details of opportunities get passed around by word of mouth. If you are known to be a reliable and honest worker, then your chances of getting a better job are good.

There is no formal career progression unless you're working for one of the big companies. Most arts and antique dealers hope one day to have their own business and premises and to expand these businesses year by year. As their own reputation grows, some move into lecturing and teaching, or acting as advisers to heritage organisations and museums.

CRAFTS

Craft workers use different materials and skills to produce objects. They may use traditional techniques that have been practised for hundreds of years, or work with modern technology. They may design and produce 'one-off' products for themselves and sell them through shops and fairs, or be commissioned to produce goods for a large business. Here are some examples of craft workers.

Blacksmith

A blacksmith uses both traditional and modern techniques to create or repair items made of different metals. This is very physical, dirty work – metals have to be melted at great heat to make them workable. There are still around 900 blacksmiths working in the UK. Artist blacksmiths produce decorative pieces such as gates and garden furniture. Industrial blacksmiths make functional objects such as tools for industry and agriculture.

Engraver

Engravers use specialist equipment to etch patterns or words onto hard surfaces such as stone, metal and glass. You'll see engraving on gravestones, trophies and decorative windows. Because new computerised machinery has made it possible for almost anyone to carry out precision engraving, the demand for skilled craftspeople has declined – but some people still make a living by producing hand-engraved goods for specialist shops and galleries. This is painstaking work that demands a lot of care and attention, but it can be enormously satisfying if you get a chance to produce and engrave your own designs.

Gold- and silversmiths

These craftspeople don't just produce jewellery – although this is an area that many choose to work in. They can also fashion small items in precious metals such as ornaments, picture frames, clocks and boxes. This job demands a high degree of skill and patience – you can't afford to make mistakes when using valuable raw materials. Smiths may work for themselves or for specialist companies or jewellery shops, producing goods to their own designs or to meet commissions from clients. There is always a demand for people who can work with gold and silver to carry out repairs to jewellery and other precious items.

Whatever the craft medium you're focusing on, your work will involve a number of different stages. If you're commissioned to produce something, you'll talk to your client to find out what they want. This will involve the following.

► Asking them to think about how the item will be used and what properties it needs. For example, if somebody asks you to make a table, its size, design and the materials you use will be influenced by what the table is going to be used for.

- ▶ Researching existing designs to find inspiration for your own ideas, and experimenting with materials and techniques.
- ▶ Sketching out ideas and producing designs, then checking that these meet with your client's approval.
- ▶ Sourcing the materials you need, preparing them, then making the object and finishing it.

Hopefully your client will like it – at which point you'll be able to give them an invoice and get paid for all your hard work.

Many craftspeople are self-employed, so as well as making items, they also run their own businesses. This means doing a lot of administrative work such as preparing budgets, doing the accounts, publicising their work, maintaining a website, packaging and delivering finished goods, checking that appropriate health and safety measures are in place, etc. – all of which can take a long time.

DESIGNER FASHION

Getting a break as a fashion designer can be difficult because it's hard to get your ideas into a place where they will be noticed by the fashion buyers who purchase finished garments for their stores. Most designers are university educated because higher education helps to refine their skills and gives them good contacts within the industry.

One way that you can get into the fashion industry and work your way up, however, is by starting off in production. When clothes have been designed, they have to be manufactured. Although large-scale production often takes place in countries like China where labour is cheap, there are still opportunities in this country for clothing and textile operatives. Here are some of the production openings that you could consider.

Clothing pattern cutter or grader

Pattern cutters produce patterns from designers' drawings; graders use computer-aided technology to scale the patterns to fit different sizes. Pattern cutters and graders are usually based in a clothing factory, and work as part of a team that includes designers, sewing machinists and finishers (who 'finish off' the garments).

Knitting machinist

The way in which a knitting machinist works will depend on whether they're employed in a large knitwear factory using sophisticated machinery or in a smaller workshop which uses more traditional machinery and techniques to produce specialist garments. If they work for the former, they could be controlling a number of machines – and be responsible for their maintenance. In smaller workshops, the machinists may get involved in everything from spinning the wool from fleeces to hand-knitting and finishing.

Textile operative

Textile operatives work in textile factories and manufacture products ranging from clothes to carpets. The job can involve preparing yarns that are going to be woven, sorting them if they are natural products, or chemical processing if they are synthetic. Textile operatives could also be spinning the yarn onto bobbins so that it can be woven or knitted at a later stage – or actually doing the weaving.

All of these jobs are usually factory based. If you choose one of them, you'll work regular hours, possibly in shifts. Factory environments have improved a great deal since the nineteenth century – but expect to be surrounded by heavy machinery, noise and dust!

Alternatively, consider going into fashion retailing to get your first opening in the industry. Working in a store that specialises in fashion or accessories will help you to understand how the business works, what sells and what doesn't. That can be invaluable knowledge that will stimulate your own designs.

If you're really keen to become a fashion designer at this stage, you can help yourself towards your goal by doing the following.

▶ Designing and making as much as possible and showing/selling it to friends and family.

▶ Keeping a portfolio of your work, which acts as a sort of CV.

▶ Making sure you're bang up to date with the latest trends and developments in the fashion world by reading fashion magazines.

▶ Visiting exhibitions and shows when you can so that you're aware of what's going on in the industry.

FILM, VIDEO AND PHOTOGRAPHY

If you're hoping to start work when you leave school or college, the jobs that you'll have access to in the film world are the same as those in television: you could start out as a runner or production assistant, make-up artist, sound, vision or lighting technician or video tape operator. The section on page 35 will give you an insight into these jobs. Here we're going to focus on photography because it's a career that offers a number of openings for entrants at all levels.

Photographer

We see the work of professional photographers every day in magazines and newspapers, on advertising billboards and internet sites. Photographers are employed in dozens of other areas besides the media: they take images of products for large corporations, photograph crime scenes, create displays for architects – and, of course, record important events like weddings and celebrations for the general public. Even though most of us now have digital cameras, we still seek the help of a professional when there is something special for which we want a permanent record.

DID YOU KNOW?

George Eastman, an American, created the first cheap, lightweight simple camera in 1888. He called it the Kodak camera because the name was short, easy to remember and could be pronounced throughout the world.

This is one career for which there are no formal entrance qualifications, although most professional photographers have completed courses to refine their talent and upgrade their technical skills. The most important factor in starting out as a photographer is to have an 'eye' for images and to instinctively know what works in terms of composition.

Photographic technicians

Another area that offers a number of employment opportunities is on the processing side. Although the days of working in a darkroom and manually developing pictures are long gone, there is still a demand for photographic technicians who print images or convert them into a digital format. They work in labs using computerised facilities and need a high degree of technical expertise.

Depending on the type of work they specialise in, technicians may:

▶ use computers to print and manipulate digital images

▶ scan and convert images into digital media

▶ mount and laminate images for exhibitions and displays.

The processing side is worth considering even if your aim is to be a photographer. It is an area in which there is a demand for skilled workers and, most importantly, it will help you to understand what makes images work.

Photographic stylist

A third career that you could consider, particularly if you're not planning on continuing your studies, is that of a photographic stylist. They work with photographers, art directors, lighting technicians and set builders to create a particular look during a photographic shoot. Their work includes:

- ▶ carrying out research and contributing ideas for the shoot
- ▶ finding props and locations
- ▶ arranging the set and background
- ▶ dressing models or laying out products so they create the desired effect.

Successful stylists often specialise in a particular area such as fashion, interior design or food photography, where they build up a reputation. If a photographer finds a stylist that they work well with, they will use them for a lot of their work.

Although there are no set qualifications for stylists, many of them have a background in art and design, or have studied photography or photographic styling. Most stylists learn 'on the job', picking up the tricks of the trade by working with more experienced colleagues. You may spend a lot of time working on location – so this isn't a job for someone who wants to be home by 6 p.m. every night.

Salaries for photographers, technicians and stylists vary enormously. When you're starting out, particularly if you are self-employed, you may find it hard to make ends meet, but once you're established, you'll make a respectable living. Freelance specialist photographers may be paid by job or by image; someone who runs a photography business on a local high street will probably have a more predictable business turnover.

SOFTWARE, COMPUTER GAMES AND ELECTRONIC PUBLISHING

These days, very few software programs and computer games are developed by solitary geeks sitting in their bedrooms. This is a valuable industry; games and software development is big business, involving established companies that are worth millions of pounds.

These companies can't afford to make mistakes and produce products that won't sell, so typically they start by carrying out extensive research into the market to see what will attract consumers. Once an idea has been put forward, various teams of designers (who decide how the game will be played or the system will operate and what it will look like) and technical experts (who create the code, animation, graphics, audio production and special effects) will work together to create the finished product. Design, programming, art and animation are the work of development studios and production houses, but products reach the public via specialist publishing companies.

> **DID YOU KNOW?**
>
> Software developers use special programming languages such as C++, Java and Assembler to develop codes for software. It is detailed, painstaking work – so you need the right sort of temperament to cope with a career in this field.

Computer technical support assistant

You're unlikely to find an opening as a software or computer games developer straight from school or college; most people take up these roles after they've studied a relevant subject at degree level (or equivalent). What you *may* be able to do is to find work as a helpdesk adviser or technical support assistant. These jobs will give you a start and help you to learn more about your chosen field.

Computer technical support assistants carry out a range of activities including installing new systems, upgrading existing ones and training staff to use them. They also solve technical problems and offer advice on how to use programs most efficiently. Many technical support assistants start out in call centres where they get used to dealing with customers over the phone and giving support to panicking technophobes!

Most large organisations employ a number of technical support assistants, so this is an area in which job prospects are usually good. There are also opportunities for promotion that could lead you into network design or more senior management posts.

Games tester

Another possible way into the games industry is to become a games tester. Companies will occasionally advertise for committed players to help them test new games' development on a voluntary basis. This offers a good grounding in the development process,

---

PROFILE

This profile focuses on Chris who has developed a career because of his passion for computer games.

Chris is a committed online games player and has been since his early teens. It's the only thing he's ever really enjoyed doing. Although academically able, he wasn't interested in academic subjects and his GCSE results were disappointing. He went to college for a year to study computer technology, which he enjoyed – but he still spent every spare minute online with his internet gaming community. Just as everyone despaired of him finding a job that he could enjoy, he got a position in France with the very company whose games he plays. His knowledge of their product, built up over a number of years, was invaluable. He started as a helpdesk assistant, has received lots of training and knows that there are good opportunities for promotion. Most importantly, he loves his work!

---

and access to software and tools. If you can then build up a relationship with the company, you may find an opening with them and get a permanent job.

Electronic publishing is a growth area, particularly as the next generation of e-readers is about to hit the market. Traditionally the creative side of publishing – choosing texts, editing, designing, etc. – has always been a highly competitive area and most people who get into this field will have a degree in a relevant subject. There are, however, openings for data processors, formatters and website designers so if you have an interest (or experience) in these areas you may be able to find an opening and work your way up the publishing ladder.

MUSIC AND THE PERFORMING ARTS

Many people are seduced by the idea of working in music, dance or the theatre because they think it's glamorous. While there is a certain magic associated with the performing arts, there's also a lot of hard work and routine, just as there is in any job. On the performance side, there is an additional challenge: there are many more would-be performers than there are openings for them.

If you want to be a singer/musician/actor/dancer/trapeze artist, etc., you'll already know the difficulties associated with getting your first break and finding paid employment – and you won't let those difficulties put you off. You'll need a combination of talent, persistence and luck – the latter is often what distinguishes successful performers from those who never make the big time.

For every performer, there are a dozen people working behind the scenes, ensuring that performances actually take place. Those are the areas that we're focusing on in this book because they offer far more opportunities for young people who are interested in careers in this field. Let's start by looking at some key jobs in the music industry.

Behind every successful (and not so successful) recording and performing artist there's an army of support workers. These are the record label and promotional staff who organise the artists' business. Here are some of them – and the work that they do.

A&R (Artists and Repertoire)

An A&R person signs up new bands and looks after the ones that have already been signed to a record label. They represent the record company to the band and they look after the band's interests within the record company. The fun part is looking at new acts and deciding whether or not they could be successful, but essentially they are business people; their work involves developing strategies to market bands and raise their profile, setting and administering budgets, and negotiating deals.

Pluggers

Without effective marketing and public relations it would be hard for any act to get its name known. Record companies usually carry out the marketing for their artists and organise all their paid-for publicity: with big-name acts, they'll spend thousands of pounds on advertising in magazines, on television and billboards.

Public relations (PR) is promotional activity that isn't paid for, such as radio and TV appearances and airplay, press reviews and interviews in newspapers and magazines.

'Plugging' is an important part of PR. It involves taking records to radio producers and DJs and persuading them to play them on air, and contacting other forms of media to ask for reviews and mentions.

Agents

Musicians' agents handle a band or DJ's gigs. They book tours and individual dates, and negotiate fees. They usually get a percentage of the money the artist earns – so the agent for a successful band can make a lot of money.

Producers and engineers

During a recording, the producer handles the creative side, arranging the songs and getting the best performances from artists whilst the engineer handles the technical side such as checking sound levels, etc. There is quite a lot of crossover between these jobs, particularly for types of music that have a high technical input like hip-hop. Many producers and engineers have their own studios and independent production companies; they hire out their services to different recording artists from different labels.

Stagehand/stage manager

No theatrical performance could take place if it weren't for the crew that works backstage – the behind scenes support staff. Depending on the size of the theatre, the backstage team may have a large number of specialists who take charge of lighting, sound, props, special effects, costumes, etc. These will be assisted by stagehands who make sure that everything is where it should be when it is needed. In small theatres, the stagehands may do a lot of the technical work themselves.

Stagehands will carry out scene changes on stage, so they have to know the exact position for furniture, equipment and props. They may move these manually or mechanically with specialist lifting equipment. They will also help to load and unload equipment, help carpenters to build and put up scenery, open and close the stage curtains, and clear and clean the stage and backstage areas.

Make-up artist

Make-up artists work in the film, stage and television industries. They are also employed by video production companies and photographers on fashion shoots. Their work varies from doing straightforward make-up and hairstyling to enhance the appearance of a television presenter, to creating special effects and making someone look totally different in age and appearance.

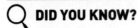

DID YOU KNOW?

One of the best-known Hollywood make-up artists is Rick Baker – who specialised in special effects and make-up for monkeys!

Most make-up artists are freelance although some are employed by large organisations such as the BBC. In a large organisation, you could work your way up the career ladder from junior or assistant make-up artist to make-up artist, and from there on to chief make-up artist or make-up designer, where you work with directors and costume designers to come up with the overall look for characters. If you're a freelance you may find it easier to get work if you're skilled in both make-up and hair styling, particularly if you are competing for contract work. The most successful freelance make-up artists may specialise in a particular type of make-up (e.g. special effects, historical drama) and will be requested by production teams who know their work.

Depending on the particular production you're working on, the hours can be long and unsociable – you'll be expected to stay on call as long as filming is going on. You may also work on location and have to spend long periods away from home.

There are some general points to remember if you're considering any career in music and the performing arts.

▶ Expect to work late nights and long, irregular hours.

▶ Theatre and venue conditions – and digs when you're on tour – are rarely luxurious. You'll spend a lot of time on the road and you may have to rough it.

▶ The industry is highly competitive and you may face periods of unemployment even when you have a lot of experience.

▶ You can't choose where you work – you must be willing to move to wherever the next job is.

▶ A good network of contacts is essential so that you know what jobs are available and have a chance of being considered for them.

► A back-up skill is useful – many people in this sector have to supplement their income by taking short-term or part-time jobs.

► Wages are low; you may earn less that £6,000 a year from your work in this sector until you're established.

TV AND RADIO

TV and radio employ thousands of people both in front of and behind the cameras. As with the performing arts, many of those who are in the limelight have been professionally trained either in drama school or in a related profession – for example, many news and current affairs presenters started their careers as journalists. There are more varied opportunities in technical and supporting roles.

Runners

Many young people get their first experience of working in TV and film as runners. Runners are employed by independent film and TV production companies, cable and satellite TV companies, the BBC and the ITV network.

Essentially runners are 'gofers' – they do basic tasks like fetching and carrying and making the tea. They report to producers or directors on a film or TV set, and to editors if they're working in post-production – although they'll also be at the beck and call of

JARGON BUSTER

Do you know what a best boy does? It's a term used in the film and TV world for the main assistant to the lighting electrician (who is also known as a gaffer). A good starting point to find out what jobs are available in TV – and to learn some of the odd names that these jobs go by – is www.startintv.com – which offers a brief description of many key roles.

other people like the cast and technical crews. The work is often ordinary and unglamorous – but runners are essential in helping the production to go smoothly.

Runners have to be willing to turn their hand to any unskilled task, from cleaning to delivering equipment to answering the phone to collecting sandwiches for the rest of the crew. As you get more experienced you could be given more responsibility and help out with administration and some technical tasks. Runners may progress to researcher jobs in television, and to become production assistants or assistant directors.

The work is badly paid, the hours are long – but it's good experience and a great way to make contacts in the industry. You may also get the chance to travel and to pick up studio skills like editing, sound mixing and production. Because a runner starts at the very bottom of the career ladder they get a thorough grounding in the industry that can help them to build up successful careers in production and directing.

There's a lot of competition for runners jobs and often they're not advertised. It's worth writing to individual production companies, sending your CV and asking them to bear you in mind if a job comes up. Be prepared to write a lot of letters.

Salaries for full-time runners start at around £10,000 a year. An experienced head runner on a major TV or film production can earn up to £20,000.

Production assistants

Production assistants help to organise the administration of television and film projects. They may be asked to carry out many different tasks, ranging from managing the production expenses to sourcing props to making travel arrangements to getting permission from a publisher to use a particular piece of music. Like runners, they are expected to turn their hand to almost anything – but their focus is primarily on administrative work.

On a large-scale project, there can be dozens of production assistants, and they may work in teams on particular aspects of the production (sound, script management and editing, props and make-up, etc.). On a smaller production you'd be expected to turn your hand to any task that needs completing.

Their working conditions and hours are just as demanding and unpredictable as those of a runner. Salaries range from around £15,250 to over £30,000 a year, depending on the scale of the production and the experience of the production assistant.

As with vacancies for runners, many are not advertised and will be passed around by word of mouth. It's worth regularly checking out websites such as www.broadcastnow.co.uk to see what's available, but it's also essential to keep writing to production companies with your details.

Video tape (VT) operators

VT operators work in production and post-production on TV programmes, including live and outside broadcasts, news bulletins and entertainment shows. Their work includes setting up and operating recording equipment, preparing material for transmission, and dubbing programmes (synchronising sounds and images).

This is demanding work; VT operators may work long shifts and unsocial hours. Depending on the size of the company they work for, they may specialise in one particular area (i.e. post-production work in the studio) or help both with filming on location and afterwards in the studio.

VT operators work with complex technical equipment so they need to be technically competent. They also need:

- ▶ good eyesight and colour vision
- ▶ to stay calm when working under pressure
- ▶ to be willing to work long hours when they are needed
- ▶ to pay attention to detail.

Although there are no set qualifications for a career in this field, you'll need some degree of technical skill and experience as well as a keen interest in video production. Increasingly new applicants for jobs have studied relevant courses at college or university, and had work experience in a related field.

Salaries range from around £15,000 to £40,000 depending on expertise and experience. Many VT operators are self-employed and work on short-term contracts.

Lighting technician

Lighting technicians look after the lighting for theatrical performances, concerts, fashion shows, advertising and photographic sets, film and TV sets – in fact, any interior or exterior area that needs lights to create a special effect. Lighting is more important to a production than many of us realise; it can be used to create a mood or feeling, and without it a scene can look very bland.

Theatre and film lighting is usually provided by specialist companies that employ technicians on short contracts. Technicians who are highly skilled and have a reputation for being reliable will often get regular contracts with a particular theatre or film/television production company.

DID YOU KNOW?

If you're a lighting technician, most of your work will be indoors, often in the afternoons, evenings and weekends when performances take place.

As well as setting up lights, technicians will operate them during a performance and maintain them when the show is over. They'll work with other engineers and backstage staff. Modern lighting rigs are usually computerised and can be very complex so the work demands a high degree of technical competence. Health and safety is a key concern, so a lot of time will be spent checking equipment and making sure that it is safe.

THE BOTTOM LINE

We've already said that most people work in the creative industries for love rather than money but you're still probably interested in the salaries that you could expect to earn. We can't give you anything more than ballpark figures here – and those figures are liable to change according to the demand for jobs and the number of people applying for them.

This chart gives a very general indication of salary ranges within the different careers sectors.

TABLE 1
SALARY RANGES IN CREATIVE INDUSTRIES

Career sector	Starting salary	Salary for experienced professionals
Art and antiques	£12,000–15,000	£25,000–35,000+
Crafts	Could be almost £0 when you start selling your crafts independently. £12,000–15,000 if you get a job as a skilled craftworker	£20,000–25,000+
Designer fashion	£13,000–15,000 for clothing and textile operatives	£20,000–25,000
Film, video and photography	£12,000–15,000	£25,000–35,000+ – more if you get a good reputation as a skilled operator
Software, computer games and electronic publishing	£15,000–18,000	£35,000+ for senior designers and operators

(Continued overleaf)

TABLE 1 (*Continued*)
SALARY RANGES IN CREATIVE INDUSTRIES

Career sector	Starting salary	Salary for experienced professionals
Music and the visual and performing arts	£6,000–10,000 when you're starting out – and you may have to wait on tables to pay the bills	The sky's the limit if you win *X Factor* or get discovered. For backstage professionals, £20,000–25,000.
Television and radio	£13,000–15,000	£25,000–35,000+ more if you get a good reputation as a skilled operator

CHAPTER 4
CASE STUDY 1

ELLIE POOLE

Stage manager/technician

Ellie Poole is a stage manager/theatre technician for a small touring theatre company. She's worked hard to get ahead in a very competitive field – and this is her story.

'The reason I give myself two job titles is because our company is so small – I'm really the Jill of all trades as far as putting the production on. In a larger company, you might have dedicated lighting and sound staff, set constructors and dressers, etc. but the director of this company just has me!

'My interest in theatre started when I was still at school – we had a great drama teacher and studio and I spent as much time as I could there. I was never interested in performing, though – I wanted to be backstage, so I helped out with as many productions as I could and I learned the basics about sound and lighting. After school I did a two-year BTEC National Certificate in Performing Arts. I was still spending all my spare time in the theatre; I joined the local youth theatre and I volunteered as a helper at the local arts centre so I got quite a lot of experience on different scale productions both in technical work and front of house.

'I was incredibly lucky to get an interview for this job when it was advertised because this is such a competitive field, and these days a lot of people have studied technical theatre courses at drama school. I got the job because I'd had a wide range of practical experience and I could turn my hand to many different types of work – set-building, lighting, etc. Also, I think the people interviewing me recognised that I was strictly backstage – I wasn't trying to get theatre work in the hope of breaking into acting!

'Ours is a touring company – though we also have residencies sometimes in small theatres that last for a few weeks at a time. I sometimes work with technicians in the theatres or, if we're working at a school or some other venue, I might work alone. I source materials for and build sets, usually working on a very tight budget. Working with the director I design and sometimes operate the sound and lights. During a performance I'm in charge of the backstage areas, make sure that props are in the right place and sets get changed and dressed quickly.

'The hours are long and the work is physically demanding so you need plenty of stamina. If we're on tour, I go into the theatre about 2 p.m. and I'll still usually be there at 11 p.m. – first in and last out! There's always something that needs repairing or replacing; then before the performance I set up the stage and make last-minute checks to make sure everything is where it should be. We're usually rehearsing another production so at the end of the evening I clear the stage ready for the next day's rehearsals.

'You've got to love this work to cope with the hours and the pay – theatre work is notoriously badly paid and it doesn't give you enough time off to get a second job. On the plus side, everyone you work with is usually as committed as you are so we have a lot of fun, and there is no place that I've found as exciting as being backstage in a theatre. There's an incredible buzz when a performance starts – you've got to experience it to know what it's like.

'If you're interested in this type of work, you have to be prepared to fight for work – there aren't a lot of jobs, and many companies have recently had their budgets cut so there are even fewer opportunities at the moment. You must also accept that the salaries are low and many people start off unpaid – so be prepared for financial hardship.

'I don't think this would be the ideal job for somebody who doesn't like travelling and moving around. I spend long periods of time away from home, living in digs when we're on tour. Even though we're a tight-knit group and all good friends, I sometimes miss my family and my friends outside the industry. And my boyfriend has had to get used to me being away, which isn't ideal.

'If you're prepared for the downsides, then they are easier to cope with. In terms of making yourself more employable, I think it helps to build up your skills base, particularly in practical things like woodwork, electrical repairs and using sound equipment. The more skills you can offer a theatre manager, the more likely you are to get a job. You must be prepared to continue upgrading your qualifications – these days there are so many regulations relating to the backstage area, health and safety, etc. that you need pieces of paper to prove that you can do even quite simple tasks; I'm collecting quite a lot of skills certificates and licences – but they're all useful.'

FIND OUT MORE...

If you want more information about courses and training for a career in the performing arts, look at the website for the National Council for Drama Training at www.ncdt.co.uk

CHAPTER 5
TOOLS OF THE TRADE

In Chapter 3, we looked at some of the jobs you could consider in the creative industries. It's a small sample – but hopefully it will have given you some ideas for your own career. In this chapter, we're going to consider the skills and attributes you'd need to succeed in these jobs: technical skills, business skills and personal qualities.

Even if your chosen career isn't featured here, you'll still find this chapter useful because it gives a broad indication of competences that applicants need to work in a particular sector. So, for instance, if you've set your heart on being a theatrical costume designer, look at the section on music and the visual and performing arts; this will tell you something about the sector and the sort of people who succeed in it.

You will notice that not every job we look at in this sector requires all three types of skills. Some jobs are part of a large organisation where the business skills would only be applicable to the boss of the company. That being said, remember that you should try to make yourself aware of how any business works so that you can broaden your understanding of the industry you're interested in.

ARTS AND ANTIQUES

If you ask a dozen people in the art and antiques trade how they started their careers, they will probably give you a dozen different answers. If you want to work for one of the big name auction houses you'll need a degree in a relevant subject such as history of art so that you can apply for a graduate internship that will teach you about different parts of the business.

There are opportunities for non-graduates – but don't make the mistake of thinking that working in this sector is an easy option. You'll need a wide range of skills, knowledge and abilities including the following.

Technical
- ▶ Knowledge about your field of art or antiques.

Business
- ▶ Good communication skills so that you can work with customers.
- ▶ Excellent negotiating skills – you need to buy your stock at the best possible price.

Personal qualities
- ▶ Stamina – the hours can be very long. As well as selling goods in a shop or a fair, you'll have to find new stock, and that can involve a lot of travelling.
- ▶ Self-discipline, particularly if you work for yourself. You will always be working, always looking for goods that could be valuable to your business.
- ▶ A willingness to continue studying in your own time, either by reading books or going on short courses to increase your knowledge of your chosen field.

Most importantly you need what the British Antique Dealers' Association calls 'flair': 'a magic ingredient ... which really marks a good dealer on any level. Flair goes beyond knowledge and experience and implies discernment, an artistic eye, enthusiasm and perhaps a dash of salesmanship; it is an innate quality which can lift a dealer out of the ordinary, whether he operates from a market stall or a shop in Bond Street'.

CRAFT WORKERS

If you're planning a career as a craftsperson, the first thing you need is to be passionate about the craft that you're going to practise. It's no good thinking you can be a carpenter specialising in high-quality furniture if you're not really interested in working with wood and getting your hands dirty! Here are some of the skills and knowledge you'll need if you're going to succeed.

Technical
- ▶ Design skills – you'll need a good 'eye' for shape, form and colour.
- ▶ Aptitude in your chosen craft.
- ▶ Good hand-eye coordination, particularly if you're working with delicate materials.
- ▶ Knowledge of craft equipment and techniques relevant to your particular field.
- ▶ The ability to read complicated designs and 'translate' them from paper into a finished article.
- ▶ Physical strength if you're working with heavy materials like wood, stone or metal.
- ▶ Understanding of materials and their properties so that you know how to work with them to achieve a particular effect.

Business
- ▶ Project management skills – you may be in charge of every stage of production, from buying raw materials to delivering the finished item.
- ▶ Communication skills so that you can discuss commissions and interpret them accurately.
- ▶ Negotiation skills so that you can get a good price for your goods – and a good price when you're buying raw materials from your suppliers.
- ▶ Administrative skills – particularly if you're self-employed and you have to manage your own finances and paperwork.

▶ Knowledge of health and safety and other legal requirements for running a business.

▶ IT skills – these will be useful when you're researching a commission or running a website to publicise your work.

Personal qualities

▶ Patience – making fine articles can be a slow and delicate process.

▶ The ability to work for long periods on your own – many craftspeople need peace and quiet to get their work done, so they work alone or in very small workshops.

▶ Confidence – you may go for long periods without commissions and this can be hard to deal with.

DESIGNER FASHION

Becoming a fashion designer isn't easy but, as we suggested in Chapter 2, one way you can get started in the industry is to consider starting out in clothes manufacture or retail to develop your skills and find out what customers want. To be a clothing or textile operative, you'll need the following skills.

Technical

▶ Good mechanical skills and manual dexterity.

▶ A good eye for colour and design.

Personal qualities

▶ To be interested in clothing and textiles and how they are made.

▶ The ability to work fast and under pressure to meet deadlines.

▶ To pay attention to detail.

▶ Able to do repetitive work.

▶ Physically fit – these jobs can be very demanding.

Once you start designing clothes – whether you're doing it in your spare time or have started to work full-time as a freelance designer – you'll need a range of skills.

Technical skills

▶ A genuine flair for design and an ability to translate your ideas onto paper and then into textiles or other materials.

▶ A good eye for colour and texture and how these work together.

▶ The ability to make clothes. Although most fashion designers use manufacturers to make up their clothes, most of them will tell you that cutting and needlework skills are important in creating realistic designs that can be easily made up.

▶ Knowledge of textiles and other materials that you will use in your designs.

Business skills

These are the same as for craft workers and for anyone who is contemplating running their own business, so refer back to the previous section. Good networking skills are also essential.

Personal qualities

▶ Dedication – this is such a competitive area that you'll need to be determined to succeed.

▶ Persistence – few people are 'discovered' overnight, and you might spend years working in junior positions before you achieve success.

▶ Stamina – fashion designers work long hours, particularly when they're preparing a new collection. They may travel a lot, too, to attend shows and trade exhibitions.

▶ Flexibility – trends change all the time and you can't afford to get set in your ways. You'll need to continually research the influences on your customers and think about what's going to happen in the future rather than what is happening now.

FILM, VIDEO AND PHOTOGRAPHY

If you're planning to work in film or video-making, read the section in this chapter on TV and radio, where we've included information about the skills and competences that will get you noticed as a runner, production assistant, technician, etc.

Successful photographers have a talent for taking pictures; they know how to combine colour, shape, pattern and form to create a particular effect. Although this skill can be taught, to a certain extent, nobody can give you the photographer's 'eye'. You either have it, or you don't.

Many photographers are self-employed, so they also need to have the motivation and the business skills to run a business, generate work and keep on top of the administration.

Photographic technicians usually work with computerised systems and need a high degree of technical competence.

Like photographers, many photographic stylists are self-employed so business skills are also important. They may have close ties with particular advertising, media and design agencies that come to rely on them and commission them regularly. A good reputation is very important – and to maintain that you need to be reliable, adaptable and hard-working.

If you're planning a career as a photographer, technician or stylist you'll need the following skills.

Technical
- ▶ Computer literacy and technical skills so that you can use the latest technology.
- ▶ A good eye for what makes a good picture.
- ▶ Understanding of photography and lighting.

Business
These are the same as for anyone who is contemplating running their own business, so refer back to the previous section on craft workers.

Personal qualities

▶ A good communicator. If you're photographing people, you need to make them comfortable in front of the camera – and that's not always easy.

▶ Self-confident and convinced of your talent so that you can persuade customers to use your services.

▶ To be able to work under pressure – images often need to be processed quickly.

▶ Painstaking in your work, attentive to detail.

▶ Be an excellent teamworker and have a lot of patience – you will be dealing with a lot of different people ranging from models to technicians, all of whom will make demands on your time and energy.

SOFTWARE, COMPUTER GAMES AND ELECTRONIC PUBLISHING

There are certain skills and aptitudes that you'll need for any job in this sector.

Technical skills

▶ Most importantly, you'll need good technical knowledge, with some programming skills at least at 'scripting' level and awareness of the various games platforms and technologies. Few companies have the resources to take on complete beginners, so they'll look for candidates who have studied IT at school and college and have at least learned the basics.

Personal qualities

▶ Good communication skills. Software and games designers usually work in teams and have to be able to communicate their vision to the artists, programmers, producers and marketing staff.

▶ Originality and creativity – it's your job to come up with new, exciting ideas.

▶ To pay close attention to detail and to work accurately, even when you're under pressure.

▶ To genuinely love working with computer technology – you're going to spend most of your working life at your workstation!

Although there are plenty of opportunities in this sector, there is also a lot of competition for the more interesting, creative jobs. Consequently, employers can afford to be selective and will often ask for minimum educational and practical qualifications, so if you can continue your education it would be wise to do so. A degree, foundation degree or HNC/D will be the minimum entry level with many companies.

MUSIC AND THE VISUAL AND PERFORMING ARTS

Although some successful performers are 'discovered' via youth theatres and open castings, nearly all of them enter the industry after training at music, drama or dance school, or at university. For backstage staff there is a wider range of routes; many start at the bottom and work their way up, learning the skills they need on the job and taking vocational courses when they need them to give them the relevant professional qualifications.

We're highlighting two jobs in the performing arts to see what skills you'll need to succeed. You should also look at the section on TV and radio because there is some crossover between these sectors.

Stagehands/stage managers

If you want to work backstage in the theatre, be prepared for long hours and low pay – this is a competitive industry that many people want to work in. Neither is it a short cut to stardom – if you really want to be a performer, you should get the right sort of training and aim for that, not try to slip in through the back door!

Here are some of the skills and knowledge you'll need if you're going to succeed backstage.

Technical

▶ Knowledge of health and safety procedures.

▶ Knowledge of manual handling techniques.

▶ Woodworking, carpentry or DIY skills are useful.

▶ An understanding of theatre practices – how things are done backstage.

Personal qualities

▶ A passion for the theatre.

▶ Physical strength and stamina – this is hard work involving a lot of lifting and running around.

▶ A good head for heights.

▶ To be prepared to work unsociable hours.

▶ To be versatile – willing to turn your hand to almost anything.

▶ To be happy to do mundane jobs like cleaning.

▶ To be calm – theatres can be stressful places, especially just before a performance.

Make-up artists

Make-up artists often start their careers by completing make-up, beauty therapy or hairdressing courses and getting experience in beauty and hair salons before going on to specialise in stage make-up.

If you're interested in a career as a make-up artist, you'll need a combination of technical skills and creative instinct. You should be prepared for a degree of uncertainty in your career; many make-up artists are freelance and don't always work consistently. Here are some of the qualities that will help you to succeed as a make-up artist.

Technical

▶ Excellent colour vision.

▶ Knowledgeable about make-up and hair products – these change frequently and you'll need to keep abreast of the latest techniques.

▶ Creative so that you can come up with ideas for make-up.

Business

▶ If you work as a freelance you'll be responsible for your own accounts and paperwork.

▶ Knowledge of health and safety and other legal requirements for running a business.

Personal qualities

▶ Good with people – you may have to deal with some nervous and highly-strung performers.

▶ Stamina – you may work long hours and you'll be on your feet most of the time.

TV AND RADIO

The jobs we describe here are also found in the film industry.

Runners

There are no specific qualifications for becoming a runner – you'll get a job through persistence and enthusiasm. What is important is that you have a lot of common sense and the ability to take orders and solve problems. A good general education is essential and you'll need excellent organisational skills.

If you've got some knowledge of the production process and relevant experience (for example in making videos as part of your studies) it may give you an edge over other applicants. You may also be able to get a place on a production course, although entrants for these are often already working in the industry.

Technical skills

▶ Any TV or film experience will be useful, particularly if it relates to the type of production you're working on.

▶ General qualifications can be useful. For example, you'll need a driving licence if you're going to be running errands. On a small production, it can help if you have experience preparing food and are IT literate because you'll be able to work with less supervision.

Personal qualities

To get a job as a runner you'll also need to be:

▶ passionate about working in TV/film production

▶ flexible and willing to turn your hand to anything

▶ energetic – you'll need a lot of stamina

▶ a good communicator and team worker – you'll be working with lots of different people

▶ able to cope with pressure and not panic

▶ uncomplaining – your role is to be seen but not heard

▶ happy to work long hours when you are needed

▶ able to cope with an uncertain career – most runners work on short contracts and may not have regular employment.

Production assistant

Many production assistants have started off as runners and worked their way to a position of more responsibility. Although you don't need any particular qualifications for this type of work, it's useful if you have some background in the industry. You could study film production at college or university, and there are a number of short courses that will give you the basics in areas such as location filming or continuity. Major broadcasting organisations such as the BBC sometimes offer new entrant schemes – but competition for places on these is very fierce. It will help if you have the following skills.

Business

▶ Time management skills – you may have a lot to do and you need to be able to prioritise the tasks and meet tight deadlines.

▶ Communication and teamworking skills.

▶ IT skills.

▶ Basic financial management and book-keeping.

Personal qualities
To be a production assistant you'll need the qualities of a runner plus you'll need to be:

▶ organised – a lot of your work will be office based and you may be managing budgets and other paperwork

▶ reliable – you'll be the sensible, calm member of the team when others are exhausted and panicking!

Lighting technician

This is a job that you can move into if you have worked previously as an electrician and have relevant qualifications. There are now specialist college courses such as the National Diploma in Technical Theatre, but the majority of 'sparks' are electricians who are passionate about TV, film, theatre, etc. To be a lighting technician, you'll need a combination of skills and knowledge.

Technical

▶ Knowledge of lighting techniques and effects.

▶ Knowledge of lighting equipment and its function.

▶ Knowledge of health and safety issues relating to lighting.

▶ An aptitude for electrical work and electronics.

Personal qualities

▶ Creative flair so that you can visualise what effect lighting will have.

▶ Good teamworking and communication skills.

▶ Be able to work quickly, often under pressure.

▶ Stamina – you may work long hours in uncomfortable conditions backstage or on a film/TV set.

▶ A head for heights – you'll be climbing up rigs many feet above the ground!

We've only looked at a few of the many jobs you could pursue in the creative industries – but hopefully they have given you an idea of the range of technical, personal and business skills you'll need to carve out your own career.

CHAPTER 6
FAQs

In this chapter, we answer some frequently asked questions that have been asked by young people who want a career in the creative industries. The first questions relate to three of the most popular sectors – the performing arts, television and designer fashion. The final questions are about getting vital work experience in your chosen field and more general aspects of working in the creative industries.

Q **I want to get into the production side of television but I know that there's a lot of competition for vacancies. What can I do to increase my chances of getting in?**

A First of all, investigate the types of job that are available – reading this book may have given you some ideas and you should also visit the Film and Television Freelance Training (FT2) website at www.ft2.org.uk. If you're thinking about general rather than technical production work (i.e. being a production assistant rather than, for example, a lighting technician) you'll find that experience of administrative work is an advantage. Think about getting work experience or a summer job in an office where you can learn basic organisational procedures and techniques. Some schools and colleges have their own film or TV production companies and you should certainly be a member and regularly volunteering to help out. Any broadcasting experience will look good on your CV, so think about volunteering for hospital or student radio or gaining work experience on a local or community radio station.

I'm desperate to work backstage in the theatre. Where should I look for jobs?

 Getting a break in the theatre isn't easy – but there are openings if you persist and look in the right places. Start by sending out letters and copies of your CV to any theatre companies in the geographical area where you want to work. Try to get the name of the stage manager before you write and address correspondence directly to them rather than sending out a circular letter 'Dear Sir or Madam'! Don't expect a lot of responses but do ask them to keep your name and details on their files. Vacancies may be advertised in the trade press such as *Broadcast, The Stage* and *Stage, Screen & Radio* magazines. Check the internet regularly by Googling for the type of job you're looking for '+vacancies' and bookmark the sites. The more experience you can get in your chosen field the better – so offer your services voluntarily to amateur companies while you are job-hunting. You never know who'll see your work!

 I've always enjoyed making jewellery and have sold some of my pieces to family and friends. My ambition is to become a jewellery designer and maker and sell my work to the general public. How can I get started?

 Congratulations on selling some of your jewellery – you've already started your career! Now you need to widen the scope of your marketing by getting in touch with a wider audience. There are a number of websites where you can set up a 'shop window' and sell your stuff.

Etsy (www.etsy.com) is an American website that provides an online marketplace for artists and crafters to sell handmade goods. When you sign up as a seller, you'll get your own online shop that you can customise with a banner and set policies for. You don't need any technical know-how to get up and running. There are small fees for listing items and you pay a commission to Etsy on every sale. An equivalent British website is www.folksy.com. This also supports original craft and design talent by showcasing work and providing a sales platform. Again, you can open your own online 'shop' and pay commission on sales.

You could also consider getting experience in retailing, say in a craft or jewellery shop, so that you can improve your retail skills and learn how to organise a shop.

Q **You say that volunteering can be a good way to get experience in a particular career. How do I go about becoming a volunteer?**

A Volunteers, especially in the creative and cultural sectors, are the life-blood of organisations; without them, many organisations couldn't function. If you know where you want to work (e.g. your local theatre, stately home, etc.) make a direct approach by phoning and then writing in to find out what opportunities might be available. Otherwise, you can get information about volunteering in your area by looking at the following websites:

- ▶ Volunteering England www.volunteering.org.uk
- ▶ Volunteering Scotland www.volunteerscotland.org.uk
- ▶ Volunteering Northern Ireland www.volunteering-ni.org
- ▶ Volunteering Wales www.volunteering-wales.net

You can also consult Do-it, the national database of volunteering opportunities (www.do-it.org.uk). Enter your postcode and areas of interest, and you will be provided with a list of potential opportunities in your local area. When you've found the organisation you want to volunteer with, you will probably need to complete an application form and have an interview. Take this seriously and prepare for it well, just as you would do for paid work.

Q **An art gallery has offered me a job for six months. I like the sound of the work and it would give me valuable experience – but it's unpaid. I know that there are a lot of people fighting for openings like this but it will be a struggle financially and I'm not sure I should take it. Any advice?**

A Unpaid 'work experience' can be a good way of getting started in your chosen field, particularly if it doesn't go on for too long and your employer genuinely intends to train you. There are, however, some unscrupulous employers who take advantage of the popularity of work in their sector. They regularly take on new recruits, expect them to work at very routine and menial tasks and offer no training at all. Only you can judge whether your offer is worth taking but try to get answers to the following questions before you make a decision.

▶ What will the work involve?
▶ Will you be given structured training that covers different aspects of the business?
▶ Will you have a mentor to advise and guide you?
▶ Is there any chance that the job will be converted into a paid post at a later date?

Think carefully about how you will finance this six-month period if you accept the job – who will support you? Is there any way you could work in the gallery part-time so that you can take paid work as well? And good luck!

 What are salaries like in the creative industries? Will I earn a good wage?

 That's a very hard question to answer because the range of careers is so great. Like any industry, when you start out you won't be earning a fortune but as your skills and experience increase, so will your earnings. Salaries tend to be on the low side for new recruits simply because there are more people wanting to work in the creative industries than there are vacancies. However, pay in the computer games and software development sector can be good. Once you're established, particularly if you gain a reputation as a talented lighting technician/photographer/make-up artist/furniture restorer, etc., then you should earn a respectable living. Look at the salary guidelines for different sectors in Chapter 3, 'The Bottom Line', p. 39.

Q **What's a typical working day?**

A That depends on what area you're working in. Most people employed in the creative industries will tell you that they quickly learn to be flexible about things like working hours. They often work on short contracts and to tight deadlines, so will sometimes work round the clock. Few of the creative industries involve structured 9 a.m. to 6 p.m. routines – but if you're enjoying yourself, you won't care! Similarly, there tend to be fewer rules and regulations than you'll find in large offices and retail outlets. You're unlikely to wear a uniform; employers will be more interested in your creative talent than your appearance. Having said that, the creative industries are no place for slackers. You'll be expected to work hard, show willingness, follow instructions and be a good team player.

How could my career progress?

The creative industry sector is one where you have to start at the very bottom and work your way up. This can take a long time, but it's an industry where you have to build up lots of experience before you can expect to work in a high level job. In many sectors, there is the opportunity to train as you work which would improve your chances of promotion. The great thing about working your way up the career ladder in this sector is that you will work alongside experienced professionals who will teach you their own expertise. This means you get the chance to see exactly what your job could progress to from the moment you start in the industry.

Are there any other opportunities?

Due to the spontaneous nature of the creative industries you will have to learn to grab opportunities as they arise. You may get the opportunity to travel, especially if you're working for a film or drama company or as a photographic stylist, as you could be sent to shoot on some amazing locations.

These are just a few questions that we've been asked. Remember that talking to people in your chosen employment sector is the best way to get the information that you'll need. In Chapter 8, we're going to look at the main training and qualifications for the creative industries, but first here is another success story.

CHAPTER 7
CASE STUDY 2

NEELA

Picture framer/restorer

Neela specialises in picture framing and restoration. She works for
a small company that has two retail outlets as well as a workshop.

'I always loved art – it was the only subject at school that I really
excelled in. Like a lot of kids, I used to dream that my talent would
be discovered and I'd be able to make my living as a fine artist –
but I was realistic enough to know that it was just a dream. I did
well in my GCSEs, and got good grades in Art and Design and
CDT, then stayed on to complete my A levels in Fine Art, History
and General Studies. I didn't go to university – I really wasn't
academic and I didn't want to study theory, so I went into the job
market when I was 18.

'As a stopgap, I took a job for a few months in a local shop – and
next door there was a picture framer and art materials store. I got
to know the owner and spent quite a lot of time watching him
work. His business was expanding and he eventually took me
on as a retail assistant and sort of apprentice framer. Right from
the beginning I loved the work because there's a strong creative
element in it. You not only need the technical skill to craft frames,
you also need an eye for colour and design so that you can show a
piece of work off to its best advantage. Most customers don't have
a clue about how a coloured mount or a decorated frame can affect

the way that their pictures look and I get a real kick out of helping them to make the best of their art works.

'At first I split my time between serving customers in the shop and making frames in the workshop. Gradually, though, I spent more of my time behind the scenes. I learned the trade purely through working with my boss – he taught me everything I needed to know.

'Occasionally someone would bring in an old painting or print that needed reframing and that made me think about conservation and restoration. I remember a lady bringing in an oil painting that was thick with dirt and sending her to the local museum to see if they could help her find someone to clean it up – and thinking that I'd like to be that person! I talked to my boss, and he encouraged me to research courses that would teach me the basics. I took a City & Guilds Creative Skills Certificate in Picture Restoration, which gave me the basic skills, then completed a City & Guilds Creative Skills Certificate in Picture/Frame Conservation/Restoration. It's very skilled work and we use a lot of powerful chemicals so there was a lot to learn, but I can now assess a picture and decide whether I can successfully clean and restore it.

'Neither framing nor restoration are jobs for people who don't have a lot of patience. It can take hours to clean a small area of a canvas – if you try to hurry the work you can destroy the picture. Similarly, framing demands close attention to detail. I also have to pay a lot of attention to health and safety because I'm working with cutting and grinding equipment and hazardous substances.

'I'm still working for the same company and I do the restoration work for both our branches. The wages are not great – they're on a par with most retail salaries. I started on £10,000 a year and now I earn more than £20,000 – but that's not a fortune by today's standards. But I love my job because I get the chance to work with beautiful things and to bring them back to their original glory. I'd rather earn less and enjoy my work.

'The promotion prospects are non-existent with my current employer. In a couple of years I may think about going back to college or university and studying conservation and restoration. With a degree and the experience I've already gained, I'd be qualified to look for work in a museum, art gallery or stately home. Who knows – I could even go freelance and set up my own picture restoration business.'

CHAPTER 8
TRAINING AND QUALIFICATIONS

We've looked at a wide range of jobs in the creative industries, focusing on those where you don't necessarily need a lot of academic qualifications. For almost all jobs, however, you'll need some sort of training, so in this chapter we'll look at some of the opportunities that are available.

CREATIVE APPRENTICESHIPS

Creative Apprenticeships offer a route into the creative industries that's based on ability and potential rather than your academic track record, background and contacts. These apprenticeships are funded by the government and specialise in training young people (16+) for careers in the creative and cultural industries. You will go to work in an organisation as a regular member of staff, but you will also receive training and have a mentor who you can turn to for help.

Apprenticeships combine 'on the job' learning and training with opportunities to acquire skills and knowledge and get industry-approved qualifications while doing so. The great thing about getting a place on a scheme like this is that it will give you a chance to get real work experience that will be important when you start looking for a job. With a Creative Apprenticeship you'll gain:

- a vocational qualification at level 2 or 3
- a theory-based qualification at level 2 or 3
- key skills in maths and English.

The range of areas in which Creative Apprenticeships are offered includes:

- promoting, organising and running live events
- the music business (focusing on the recording industry)
- technical theatre (this covers rigging, lighting and sound operations)
- costume and wardrobe
- cultural and heritage venue operations
- community arts management.

Every apprenticeship is different because the way in which it is delivered will depend on the employer who takes you on, but it will enable you to get some professional qualifications. Also, the government-sponsored apprenticeship schemes change from year to year so it's essential that you check out the latest information on www.ccskills.org.uk.

There are many other apprenticeships available besides those in the creative industries that might be relevant to your chosen career. For example, if you have plans to be a craft engineer, you may be able to find an apprenticeship that will give you formal

PROFILE

In January 2007 Davide Sgorbati took part in a pilot scheme for Creative Apprenticeships. He was contracted to work for a UK record label for four days a week for a 10-month period. His experience included working on administration and public relations, marketing and organising events. He even went on a five-week tour to promote unsigned bands and artists. When his apprenticeship finished, the company offered David a full-time job. (Adapted from www.ccskills.org.uk)

qualifications while you train 'on the job'. For more information go to www.apprenticeships.org.uk.

DIPLOMA IN CREATIVE AND MEDIA

The Diploma in Creative and Media was launched in September 2008 and is available to 14–19 year olds in many schools across England. These are new qualifications that offer an alternative learning style to traditional qualifications like GCSEs and A levels. Diplomas are different from GSCEs and A levels because:

- ▶ you get practical experience that relates directly to working life even though you continue to learn in the classroom
- ▶ the content focuses on skills that you'll need for work, as well as theory
- ▶ you can tailor your work to reflect your own areas of interest – so, for example, if you're into music you can complete a portfolio of music-related studies.

The Diploma in Creative and Media is available at three levels:

- ▶ Foundation Diploma (equivalent to studying four or five GCSEs at grades D to G)
- ▶ Higher Diploma (equivalent to studying five or six GCSEs at grades A* to C)
- ▶ Advanced Diploma (equivalent to studying three A levels).

From 2011 there will be an Extended Diploma that contains extra maths and English plus extra additional and specialist learning. The Extended Diploma at Foundation level is the same as seven GCSEs at grades D to G; at Higher level it's worth nine GCSEs at grades A* to C, and at Advanced it's the same as four and a half A levels.

If you study for a diploma, you'll combine learning theory with practical and 'soft' skills (e.g. communication and team-working skills) that will give you the knowledge, experience and understanding you need if you're planning to go into further or higher education or into your first job. The key areas are as follows.

▶ **Creativity in context:** The things that can influence the creative process, such as society, culture, the environment or the work of other people.

▶ **Thinking and working creatively:** Ways of exploring, experimenting with and developing ideas, skills and techniques.

▶ **Principles, processes and practice:** The skills, techniques and processes to turn your ideas into reality.

▶ **Creative businesses and enterprise:** An understanding of real situations and the skills that you need to succeed in the industry.

When you've completed your first diploma, you can stay at school or college and do another course such as the next level of diploma, A levels or an NVQ which could lead into higher education and a university course. Alternatively you can look for an apprenticeship or find a job that offers further training. For more information about diplomas, go to www.skillset.org.

NVQs

NVQ stands for National Vocational Qualification, and SVQ is the equivalent in Scotland (Scottish Vocational Qualification). They are competence-based qualifications, meaning that you learn by carrying out practical, work-related tasks that help you develop the skills and knowledge you need to do a job effectively. Taking an NVQ/SVQ could be appropriate if you already have skills and want to improve them, or if you're starting from scratch.

Film and Television Freelance Training (FT2) offers training for technical and production careers. Training is job based, and includes opportunities to work towards relevant NVQs. To find out more, go to www.ft2.org.uk.

NVQs/SVQs are based on national standards for various occupations that set out what a competent person in a job could be expected to do. There are five levels in the National Qualifications Framework.

Level 1

Foundation skills

Level 2

Operative, semi-skilled tasks

Level 3

Technician, craft, skilled and supervisory tasks

Level 4

Technical, junior management skills

Level 5

Specialist skills leading to chartered professional status and senior management positions.

Both adults and young people can study for NVQs and they're suitable if:

▶ you are employed
▶ you are studying at college and have a part-time job or access to a work placement.

You can also take an NVQ qualification at level 2 or 3 as part of an apprenticeship. If you successfully complete an NVQ at level 3, you could go on to higher education course in a related vocational area, such as a:

- ▶ Higher National Certificate
- ▶ Higher National Diploma
- ▶ Foundation Degree
- ▶ or another vocational specialism.

If you're thinking of working in the creative industries there are a number of NVQs that could be useful including studies related to business and management, sales, marketing and distribution, and leisure services.

HIGHER EDUCATION

You may be considering completing a college or university course before starting work. Employers value relevant qualifications, so it's worth investigating the options for higher education related to the creative industry that you want to work in. Increasingly, workers in the creative industries are continuing their education to university level. There are hundreds of courses available, so be prepared to do some serious research to find the one that's best for you.

HNCs and HNDs

HNCs (Higher National Certificates) and HNDs (Higher National Diplomas) are work-related higher education qualifications. Whereas bachelors' degrees at university tend to focus on theory and gaining knowledge, HNCs and HNDs give you the skills to use that knowledge effectively in a particular job.

More than 400 higher education colleges and further education colleges offer HNCs and HNDs, they are highly valued by employers both in the UK and overseas, and can also count towards membership of professional bodies and other employer organisations.

If you want to work in the creative industries, there are HNCs and HNDs available in areas, such as performing arts, computing and IT and hospitality management.

You'll normally need a minimum of one A level (or equivalent) to join an HND course. Once you've completed your course you can use it to:

▶ move straight into a career

▶ progress within your current career – it could, for example, help you to gain professional status

▶ get a degree. An HNC can allow entry into the second year of a degree, while HNDs may allow entry into the second or third year.

Diploma of Higher Education

A Diploma of Higher Education is similar to an HND in that it is a professional qualification that is respected by employers and can be converted to a degree with an extra year of study. If you have a degree, you may be able to enter your chosen career at a higher level than someone who starts straight from school.

Foundation degree

Foundation degrees equip you with the skills and knowledge that businesses are looking for. You can complete them at an educational institution (a higher or further education college), through distance learning, in the workplace or online. They are broadly equivalent to the first two years of a bachelor's degree and can lead straight to a job, or prepare you for further developing your professional skills. There are approximately 1,700 courses available and more are planned – find out more about them on the UCAS website.

Bachelor's degree

If you have relevant educational qualifications, you may plan to go to university and study for a bachelor's degree. If you study full-time, a course will take three or four years; increasingly, universities are offering four-year courses that include an element of work experience.

These degree courses are designed to give you a thorough understanding of your chosen subject. There is a bewildering range of courses on offer and each institution's offer will be different to the next, so it's essential that you research the options carefully.

Entry to a degree course is usually dependent on your academic qualifications, though the demands may be relaxed for mature students. UCAS operates a system called the 'UCAS Tariff'; your previous qualifications can earn points on the tariff to get a place on a particular higher education course. To find out what is required for a course you're interested in, either read the course prospectus (most are available online) or visit the UCAS website.

Many people who move into the creative industries have been to university and studied for degrees that are not directly related to their job. For example there are very few higher education courses that would train you to be an art or antiques dealer, but studying subjects such as history, archæology or history of art will give you some useful knowledge that may provide a basis for your career.

Here are some examples of qualifications that you could study at different levels for the sectors we've looked at in this book.

TABLE 2
EXAMPLES OF RELEVANT QUALIFICATIONS

Industry sector	Some relevant qualifications
Art and antiques	City & Guilds Creative Skills Certificate in Picture Restoration NVQ/SVQ Cultural Heritage Operations NVQ/SVQ Heritage Care and Visitor Services BA Antiques and Design Studies

(Continued)

Industry sector	Some relevant qualifications
Crafts	There is a wide range of qualifications available related to individual craft areas. You could start with a City & Guilds in your chosen area and move all the way up to HNC/D or degree. We haven't given examples of specific courses here because the choice is so varied.
Designer fashion	NVQ/SVQ Manufacturing Sewn Products NVQ/SVQ Manufacturing Textiles NVQ Apparel Manufacturing Technology HNC/D Textiles Foundation Degree Textiles/Fashion Design BA Fashion Design
Film, video and photography	City & Guilds Photography NVQ/SVQ Photography NVQ/SVQ Photo Imaging/Photo Processing NVQ/SVQ Broadcast, Film and Video Production Foundation/BA Photography 14–19 Diploma IT
Software, computer games and electronic publishing	HNC/HND/ Foundation Degree/BSc Computer Games Technology/ Digital Entertainment/ Computer Science
Music and the visual and performing arts	BTEC DJ Technology/Popular Music/Music Technology NVQ/SVQ Performing Arts NVQ/SVQ Stage Management National Diploma in Technical Theatre HND/BA/BSc Technical Theatre/ Theatre Design/ Theatre Production
Television and radio	NVQ/SVQ Broadcast, Film and Video Production Foundation Degree/BA Media Studies

DID YOU KNOW?

According to the government:

- ▶ 56% of businesses facing recruitment difficulties in the creative industries said that applicants lacked the right skills for the job they were applying for.

- ▶ 33% of businesses facing recruitment difficulties in the creative industries said that applicants lacked experience.

Qualifications are important, particularly if you are competing for jobs in a crowded marketplace. However, in the creative industries, there are three other areas that are also important if you're going to get the job that you want.

- ▶ **Creative talent:** It may sound obvious but there are certain things that you can't teach everyone. You'll find it hard to succeed unless you have a genuine passion and aptitude for your chosen field.

- ▶ **An appropriate skill set:** Communication and teamworking skills are essential if you're working with other people. Anybody who plans to go freelance will need business, financial and time management skills.

- ▶ **Experience that's relevant to the job:** For employers, someone with relevant on-the-job experience is more valuable than an untested graduate.

CHAPTER 9
THE LAST WORD

This book has introduced you to just a few of the hundreds of career opportunities available in the creative industries. There are, of course, many other jobs that you could consider if you're planning to leave school or college and start work immediately, as well as hundreds of relevant training and education courses that will give you a start in your chosen sector.

Now you need to decide – is this the right sector for you? In this chapter, we'll help you to make that decision.

ARE YOU THE RIGHT PERSON?

One point that we've made over and over again is that the creative industries are highly competitive. If you choose to work in this sector:

▶ you must be confident about your own creative talent

▶ you'll have to be persistent in looking for work

▶ you may face job insecurity – periods when you are not regularly employed in your chosen job but have to 'temp' in another career area

▶ you won't earn megabucks (not until you're famous!).

On a more positive note, there are good job opportunities for the right people. Most importantly, the creative industries offer tremendous job satisfaction. If you have a driving ambition to express your talents and creativity, you won't be happy doing anything else.

You are the best judge of whether you have the qualities that you need to succeed in this sector. Hopefully this book has been a starting point and given you plenty to think about. It has given an overview of the creative industries, introduced some of the training opportunities and opened your eyes to some of the jobs you could consider. It should also have made you think seriously about whether you have the relevant personal skills and qualities that will enable you to succeed.

CHECKLIST

If you've made it this far through the book, you should know if the creative industries are really for you. Before getting in touch with the professional organisations listed in the next chapter, here's a final checklist to help you assess whether you've chosen the right career sector.

Tick yes or no

Do you have a particular creative talent about which other people have already commented positively?	☐ Yes ☐ No
Have you already started building up a portfolio of your best work?	☐ Yes ☐ No
Are you prepared to cope with financial uncertainty if your chosen job is badly paid or you have periods without employment?	☐ Yes ☐ No
Are you self-motivated and able to work on your own initiative?	☐ Yes ☐ No
Can you manage your own workload?	☐ Yes ☐ No
Are you prepared to work long hours when required?	☐ Yes ☐ No

Can you cope with setbacks like not always getting work that you've applied for?	☐ Yes ☐ No
Are you willing to subsidise your creative work by taking other part-time jobs if necessary to earn some money?	☐ Yes ☐ No

If you've answered 'Yes' to all these questions, then congratulations! You've chosen the right career sector. If you've answered 'No' to any of these questions then a creative career may not be for you. However, there are still plenty of jobs available in the creative sector that may suit you better. You could, for example, consider a career in retailing or administration with a company that is linked to your area of interest. You may not be a fashion designer – but you could have a great career managing a fashion shop!

WHERE TO START?

If you're seriously interested in one of the careers mentioned in this book, what should you do next? Here are some suggestions.

▶ Do some more research. The internet is a great starting point and will give you more information about available jobs, the people who work in different sectors and relevant training. There are internet addresses for professional organisations that can offer more advice about your chosen career in the Further Information section of this book

▶ Could you move into your chosen job area with your current training and qualifications? If not, what training do you need and where can you get it? Talk to a careers adviser. They should have information about schemes such as apprenticeships that could help you get started. Think carefully about whether you can take up a full-time training course, or would prefer to study part time and earn money at the same time. There have never been more opportunities to gain educational, vocational and professional qualifications, so make the most of them.

▶ Talk to friends, family and anyone else you know who may have contacts in your chosen sector. These are industries that rely heavily on word-of-mouth recommendations; remember that we said at the beginning of this book that *who* you know is as important as *what* you know. Your contacts could tell you more about the work you're hoping to get into and know about possible openings.

▶ Try to get some experience. There is nothing like hands-on work experience to help you find out exactly what a job is like and if you have the qualities to make the grade. Working as a road manager for a band might sound glamorous and exciting, but the reality of being on the road, working unsocial hours under continual pressure is not for everyone. Volunteer to roadie for a local amateur band so that you learn the technical ropes and get an idea of the challenges you'll face. Work experience is also one of the keys to getting a job: few employers in the creative industries have the time and resources to train absolute beginners. If you have some practical experience and skills, you are more likely to be considered when an opening arises.

▶ Start putting together a portfolio that shows off your talents. Whether you want to be a picture framer or a violinist, a dressmaker or a computer games designer, you should be able to show people examples of your work. With modern technology, maintaining a portfolio has never been easier – you can even download it to a social networking site like YouTube so it's available to anyone who wants to look at it. Better still, set up your own website!

Whatever your chosen career, there are people out there who can help you to find out more and help you succeed. In the next section, you'll find details of organisations that can help you move forward towards an interesting and fulfilling career in the creative industries.

CHAPTER 10
FURTHER INFORMATION

Listed in this section are contact details for organisations that can give you more information about careers, education and training opportunities in the creative industries. We haven't included phone numbers because a lot of the information you require will be available on websites, together with a direct contact facility.

GENERAL

Careers

For information about apprenticeships, including creative apprenticeships:
www.apprenticeships.org.uk

For information and careers advice in England:
www.connexions.gov.uk

For information and careers advice in Scotland:
www.careers-scotland.org.uk

For information and careers advice in Wales:
www.careerswales.com

For information and careers advice in Northern Ireland:
www.delni.gov.uk

Courses

For information on vocational courses, contact:
City & Guilds, 1 Giltspur Street, London EC1A 9DD
www.cityandguilds.com

For information about applications for higher education courses,
contact:
UCAS, Rosehill, New Barn Lane, Cheltenham GL52 3LZ
www.ucas.ac.uk

Creative

Arts Council of England, 2 Pear Tree Court, London EC1R 0DS
www.artscouncil.org.uk

Arts Council Northern Ireland, 77 Malone Road, Belfast BT9 6AQ
www.artscouncil-ni.org.uk

Arts Council Wales, 9 Museum Place, Cardiff CF10 3NX
www.artswales.org.uk

Creative & Cultural Skills (Sector Skills Council for advertising,
crafts, cultural heritage, the arts and music), 11 Southwark Street,
London SE1 1RQ
www.ccskills.org.uk

Scottish Arts Council, 12 Manor Place, Edinburgh EH3 7DD
www.scottisharts.org.uk

Department for Culture Media and Sport, 2–4 Cockspur Street,
London SW1Y 5DH
www.culture.gov.uk

SECTOR SPECIFIC

Arts and antiques

The British Antique Dealers' Association, 20 Rutland Gate,
London SW7 1BD, advertises vacancies in its newsletter.

Become instantly more attractive

Fine Art Trade Guild, 16–18 Empress Place, London SW6 1TT
www.fineart.co.uk

Institute of Conservation, 3rd floor, Downstream Building,
1 London Bridge, London SE1 9BG
www.icon.org.uk

The London and Provincial Antique Dealers' Association, 535
King's Road, London SW10 0SZ, offers general information and
guidance on careers in antiques.

National Association of Decorative and Fine Arts Societies,
NADFAS House, 8 Guildford Street, London WC1N 1DA
www.nadfas.org.uk

Crafts

Arts Advice
www.artsadvice.com

Crafts Council, 44a Pentonville Road, London N1 9BY
www.craftscouncil.org.uk

Design Council, 34 Bow Street, London WC2E 7DL
www.designcouncil.org.uk

Jewellery and Allied Industries Training Council, 10 Vyse Street,
Hockley, Birmingham B18 6LT
www.jaitc.org.uk

Designer fashion

Skillfast-UK (Sector Skills Council for the apparel, footwear and
textile industries) Richmond House, Lawnswood Business Park,
Redvers Close, Leeds LS16 6RD
www.skillfast-uk.org

Film, video and photography

Association of Photographers, 81 Leonard Street,
London EC2A 4QS
www.the-aop.org

British Film Institute (BFI), 21 Stephen Street, London W1T 1LN
www.bfi.org.uk

British Institute of Professional Photographers, Fox Talbot House,
2 Amwell End, Ware SG12 9HN
www.bipp.com

Film and Television Freelance Training (FT2), 3rd Floor,
18–20 Southwark Street, London SE1 1TJ
www.ft2.org.uk

National Electrotechnical Training, 34 Palace Court,
London W2 4HY

www.networks.org.uk

Skillset (Sector Skills Council for the audiovisual industries)
Prospect House, 80–110 New Oxford Street, London WC1A 1HB
www.skillset.org

UK Film Council, 10 Little Portland Street, London W1W 7JG
www.ukfilmcouncil.org.uk

www.photoassist.co.uk
This website includes an information section that is invaluable
to anyone who wants a career in photography, with sections on
compiling a portfolio, taking pictures, finding work as an assistant
and new technological developments.

Software, computer games and electronic publishing

British Computer Society, North Star House, North Star Avenue,
Swindon SN2 1FA
www.bcs.org

British Interactive Media Association, Briarlea House, Southend
Road, Billericay CM11 2PR
www.bima.co.uk

e-skills UK (Sector Skills Council for information technology),
1 Castle Lane, London SW1E 6DR
www.e-skills.com

Music and the visual and performing arts

Arts and Entertainment Technical Training Initiative, Lower
Ground, 14 Blenheim Terrace, London NW8 0EB
www.touchlondon.co.uk

Association of British Theatre Technicians, 47 Bermondsey Street,
London SE1 3XT
www.abtt.org.uk

Council for Dance Education and Training, Toynbee Hall,
28 Commercial Street, London E1 6LS
www.cdet.org.uk

Dance UK, Battersea Arts Centre, Lavender Hill,
London SW11 5TF
www.danceuk.org

Equity, Guild House, Upper Saint Martin's Lane,
London WC2H 9EG
www.equity.org.uk

Musicians Union, 60–62 Clapham Road, London SW9 0JJ
www.musiciansunion.org.uk

National Arts Youth Theatres, Darlington Arts Centre,
Vane Terrace, Darlington DL3 7AX
www.nayt.org.uk

National Council for Drama Training, 1–7 Woburn Walk,
London WC1H 0JJ
www.ncdt.co.uk

Production Services Association, Centre Court, 1301 Stratford
Road, Hall Green, Birmingham B28 9HH
www.psa.org.uk

School of Sound Recording, 10 Tariff Street,
Manchester M1 2FF
www.s-s-r.com

Stage Management Association, 47 Bermondsey Street,
London SE1 3XT
www.stagemanagementassociation.co.uk

Television and radio

BBC Recruitment, PO Box 48305, London W12 6YE
www.bbc.co.uk/jobs

Broadcasting Entertainment Cinematographic and Theatre Union
(BECTU), 373–377 Clapham Road, London SW9 9BT
www.bectu.org.uk

Channel 4 artist profiles, careers advice, training and funding
information.
www.channel4.com/4talent

Community Media Association, The Workstation,
15 Paternoster Row, Sheffield S1 2BX
www.commedia.org.uk

Cyfle, 33–35 West Bute Street, Cardiff CF10 5LH
www.cyfle.co.uk

Hospital Broadcasting Association
www.hbauk.co.uk

Independent Television Association, ITV Network Centre,
200 Gray's Inn Road, London WC1X 8HF
www.itvjobs.com

National Film and Television School (NFTS), Beaconsfield
Studios, Station Road, Beaconsfield HP9 1LG
www.nftsfilm-tv.ac.uk

Production Guild, N & P Complex, Pinewood Studios,
Iver Heath SL0 0NH
www.productionguild.com

The Radio Academy, 5 Market Place, London W1W 8AE
www.radioacademy.org

RadioCentre, 77 Shaftesbury Avenue, London W1D 5DU
www.radiocentre.org

Scottish Screen, 249 West George Street, Glasgow G2 4QE
www.scottishscreen.com

Skillset (Sector Skills Council for the audiovisual industries),
Prospect House, 80–110 New Oxford Street, London WC1A 1HB
www.skillset.org

Skillset, Focus Point, 21 Caledonian Road, London N1 9GB
Free careers helplines: 08080 300 900 (England and Northern
Ireland), 0808 100 8094 (Scotland) and 0800 0121 815 (Wales)
www.skillset.org

Student Radio Association (SRA), c/o The Radio Academy
www.studentradio.org.uk

Information on volunteering

Volunteering England, Regents Wharf, 8 All Saints Street,
London N1 9RL
www.volunteering.org.uk

Volunteer Development Scotland, Stirling Enterprise Park,
Stirling FK7 7RP
www.vds.org.uk

Volunteering Wales
www.volunteering-wales.net

Volunteer Development Agency, 129 Ormeau Road, Belfast
BT7 1SH
www.volunteering-ni.org

The National Trust, Community, Learning and Volunteering,
Heelis, Kemble Drive, Swindon SN2 2NA
www.nationaltrust.org.uk

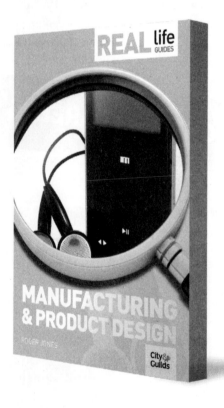